PICTURE HISTORY

OF AVIATION

ON LONG ISLAND
1908–1938

GEORGE C. DADE and
FRANK STRNAD

DOVER PUBLICATIONS, INC.
New York

To Paul Edward Garber

Published in Canada by General Publishing Company, Ltd.,
30 Lesmill Road, Don Mills, Toronto, Ontario.
Published in the United Kingdom by Constable and Company, Ltd.,
10 Orange Street, London WC2H 7EG.

Picture History of Aviation on Long Island: 1908–1938 is a new
work, first published by Dover Publications, Inc., in 1989.

Manufactured in the United States of America
Dover Publications, Inc.
31 East 2nd Street
Mineola, N.Y. 11501

Edited by Alan Weissman
Book design by Carol Belanger Grafton, CBG Graphics

Library of Congress Cataloging-in-Publication Data

Dade, George C.
Picture history of aviation on Long Island, 1908–1938 /
by George C. Dade and Frank Strnad.
p.   cm.
ISBN 0-486-26008-9
1. Aeronautics—New York—Long Island—History.
I. Strnad, Frank. II. Title.
TL522.N7D33   1989
629.13′09747′21—dc20   89-31298
                                                              CIP

ACKNOWLEDGMENTS

A book of this scope would not have been possible without the assistance of many friends of Long Island's aviation heritage. Our thanks to members of The Long Island Early Fliers Club and to Cradle of Aviation Museum volunteers who allowed us to look through their scrapbooks and suggested many additional sources of information. We are particularly grateful to all those who responded to our request for old photographs. Many photographs we would have liked to use had to be left out for lack of space. To those whose photographs could not be used, we offer our regrets and deepest thanks.

As this book goes to press, we recall with gratitude Tom Foxworth's invitation to visit his home in Virginia and photograph many of the historical pictures in his extensive files. Another pleasant memory associated with the preparation of this book is the arrival of the voluminous package from Hawaii containing Lester "Husky" Flewellin's scrapbook compiled while he was lead mechanic for the Curtiss Flying Service in Garden City in the early 1920s.

We wish to credit also the photographers whose work graces these pages. These include Henry S. Villard, Frederick J. Weber, Edwin Levick, Joseph Burt, Henry Newell, Henry Otto Korten, Luis Azarraga (better known as "Court Commercial Photo"), Rudy Arnold, and John "Scoop" Drennan. Some of these men specialized in aviation. For some it was merely a sideline. Some have become famous, others are less well known, yet others totally unknown, but all have contributed in some way to the preservation of Long Island's aviation heritage. We are also grateful to every aviation enthusiast and collector who saved old photographs which but for their efforts might have been lost.

Finally, we would like to express our gratitude to Paul Edward Garber, Historian Emeritus and Ramsey Fellow, National Air and Space Museum, Smithsonian Institution. Mr. Garber, dean of American aviation historians, graciously consented to read the manuscript for the captions in this book, and provided many helpful suggestions for its improvement. Above all, Mr. Garber, who was instrumental in acquiring the *Spirit of St. Louis* for the Smithsonian, among many other achievements, has provided inspiration and precedent for all of us who have worked to preserve our aviation heritage. Therefore, as a token of our appreciation of his accomplishment, we dedicate this book to him.

G. D.
F. S.

An Index appears on pages 169–173

ABOUT THE AUTHORS

GEORGE DADE

Better than any lengthy biographical statement, the photographs on the right illustrate the extent of George Dade's lifelong involvement in aviation. At the top, a sixteen-year-old George helps Charles Lindbergh adjust a parachute at Curtiss Field in 1928. Below, 45 years later, Dade (right) shows Lindbergh a part of the latter's original Curtiss "Jenny" (first flown by him in 1923), which had been retrieved by Dade from an Iowa farmer and was being restored by members of The Long Island Early Fliers Club for exhibit at the Cradle of Aviation Museum, of which Dade was the Founding Director. Dade lived at Curtiss Field from 1921, working part-time for the Curtiss Flying Service—and meeting world-famous pilots—while he attended high school. An active pilot himself for many years, he first soloed in 1929, when he was sixteen. Before and during World War II, he developed, with his brother, a successful business packaging and shipping aircraft around the world. In 1945 he was named by the U.S. Junior Chamber of Commerce as one of the "Ten Outstanding Young Men of the Year." More recently, working to preserve Long Island's aviation heritage, he served three terms as president of The Long Island Early Fliers Club and was the first chairman of the Cradle of Aviation Committee of the Friends for Long Island's Heritage, a National Governor of the OX-5 Aviation Pioneers, and an Associate Member of the Early Birds of Aviation. In 1979 he coauthored, with George Vecsey, *Getting off the Ground*, a book about the pioneers of aviation. In 1987 he was inducted into the Long Island Hall of Fame as "Father of Long Island's Cradle of Aviation Museum," and in 1988 received the Lawrence Sperry Award of the New York State Air Force Assocation. George Dade continues in his ardent commitment to the preservation of the aviation heritage of Long Island, where he resides with his wife Edith.

FRANK STRNAD

For half a century, Frank Strnad has been intimately associated with aviation and is now one of its most respected historians. His writings on the subject have been published internationally, and he is a consultant to authors, artists, and museums. His penchant for detail helped assure the accurate restoration of Lindbergh's "Jenny" (which he originally located) as well as the accuracy of the captions in the present book. Strnad is also a pilot, an aviation photographer, and an ardent collector of aviation memorabilia, specializing in Long Island. Many photographs from his extensive collection have been reproduced in these pages. He was employed by the Republic Aviation Corporation for 31 years, primarily in the Quality Assurance Department, and is a member of the American Aviation Historical Society, the Aircraft Owners and Pilots Association, Cross and Cockade International (Society of World War I Aero Historians), the OX-5 Aviation Pioneers, The Long Island Early Fliers Club (of which he was a trustee for twelve years), the Antique Airplane Assocation, the P-47 Alumni Association, the Aviation/Space Writers Association, the World Airline Historical Society, and the Experimental Aircraft Assocation (he is a past president of Chapter 3). He lives on Long Island with his wife Helen, and his dedication to the preservation of Long Island's aviation heritage continues. The photograph shows Frank Strnad (left) with Sherman Fairchild at a Fairchild stockholders' meeting in 1966.

INTRODUCTION

Charles Lindbergh's flight across the Atlantic in 1927 has been celebrated as one of the great events of the twentieth century and, next to the Wright brothers' first flight, is the best-known event in the history of American aviation. Most people who know of the Wrights' flight associate it with a place: Kitty Hawk, North Carolina. Lindbergh's flight is usually thought of as originating simply in "New York." Some may remember that the "Lone Eagle" took off for Paris from a place called "Roosevelt Field." Today not many of us, unfortunately, have any clear idea where Roosevelt Field was or know if it still exists. Fewer still have any real conception of the important role it played in aviation history.

Roosevelt Field is now the site of a shopping center and a racetrack in a fairly typical suburb about twenty miles east of Manhattan in Nassau County, Long Island, New York, and has been so for over thirty years; but, beginning almost eighty years ago, for a period of about thirty years, Roosevelt Field was the bustling site of some of the most spectacular advances in aviation anywhere in the world. There and at neighboring Curtiss Field and Mitchel Field (airfields also bearing other names at different times) speed and endurance records were broken, new aircraft and flying instruments tested, and outstanding flights begun and completed, many of which marked breakthroughs in technology or established new connections by air with distant places.

This area, once known as the Hempstead Plains, was created by an outwash of glacial sediment some ten thousand years ago, leaving a vast expanse of perfectly flat, open land ideally suited for experiments in flying. Aviation pioneer Glenn Curtiss was the first to recognize the potential of the Hempstead Plains when he moved his base of flying operations there in 1909. Within months it was established as a center of aeronautical activity that was to continue under military auspices through the First World War. After the war, civilian flying activities were resumed and continued on a broad scale, side by side with the military, for another twenty years, when such activities began to be moved elsewhere. Meanwhile, other parts of Long Island had begun to share the glory of achievement in aviation.

All things considered, Long Island proved to be ideal for experiments in flying with powered machines. Large tracts of land were available. Its location, about halfway between Europe and the Pacific Coast, was a natural starting or terminal point for both transcontinental and trans-Atlantic flights. Furthermore, no place on Long Island is very far from water, providing a number of sites for the testing and flying of seaplanes. Adjoining and partly coextensive with heavily populated New York City, Long Island was also a natural source of skilled labor for the aeronautical industry. Its airfields were convenient to the many budding aviators in the metropolitan area (among whom was one of the present authors, George Dade). And it provided large, enthusiastic audiences for the many flying competitions held in early days, as well as for many of the most sensational record-breaking flights.

Long Island is a very large island indeed, comprising four counties, two of which, Kings and Queens, are also boroughs (Brooklyn and Queens) of New York City. To the east of Queens lies Nassau County and then Suffolk County, stretching about ninety miles to the tip of Montauk Point. Although the Hempstead Plains, in the middle of Nassau (see the map on pages viii and ix), was the major site of flying achievement for some twenty years, the first flight on Long Island (simultaneously the first in New York City) was at the Brighton Beach Race Track in Brooklyn in 1908. A large number of other important flights were also made to, from, or in Brooklyn at Brighton Beach, at the Sheepshead Bay Speedway, and, in the 1930s, at Floyd Bennett Field. In Queens, Far Rockaway, the starting point for the first trans-Atlantic flight, and North Beach Airport also saw important flying activity. Queens was a center of aircraft manufacturing as well, beginning in 1917 at the L. W. F. factory in College Point. Nassau eventually surpassed Queens as a manufacturing center, with the plants of Curtiss, Grumman, Sperry, and many others. There was also significant aeronautical activity at many other airfields in Nassau, most notably Curtiss Field in Valley Stream. In the period treated here, 1908–1938, Suffolk County was far less prominent as an aviation center, but during the war there was significant military flying activity at the Bay Shore Air Station on Great South Bay, and a number of other aeronautical activities were pursued over the years at locations from Amityville on the Nassau border, all the way out to the Montauk Naval Air Station, a dirigible base near the extreme eastern tip of Long Island.

The concentration of so much achievement in American aviation on Long Island in those pioneering days made it truly the "cradle of aviation," as it has been called. Even to this day, research and manufacturing for the aerospace industry go on, demonstrating Long Island's continuing role in this field. Yet somehow the standard histories of aviation have missed noticing all this, even while they recount numerous events that did in fact take place on Long Island. It is no wonder that so few people are aware of Long Island's central place in aviation history.

One reason for the present book is to fill this historical gap. We have here assembled several hundred archival photographs from various sources, constituting a fascinating record of aviation on Long Island in the crucial three decades from 1908 to 1938, including many magnificent contributions to man's on-going attempt to conquer the sky. You will find here photographs not only of a triumphant Charles Lindbergh and his *Spirit of St. Louis* but also of many other great aviators, innovative airplanes, and scenes of startling achievement, as well as a record of well-meaning failures and curiosities, and of the exciting everyday activities that made Long Island's airfields the focus of so much eager attention in those wonderful years. We hope these pictures and our words will contribute to the preservation of the glorious heritage of that time.

HEMPSTEAD PLAINS AIRFIELDS:

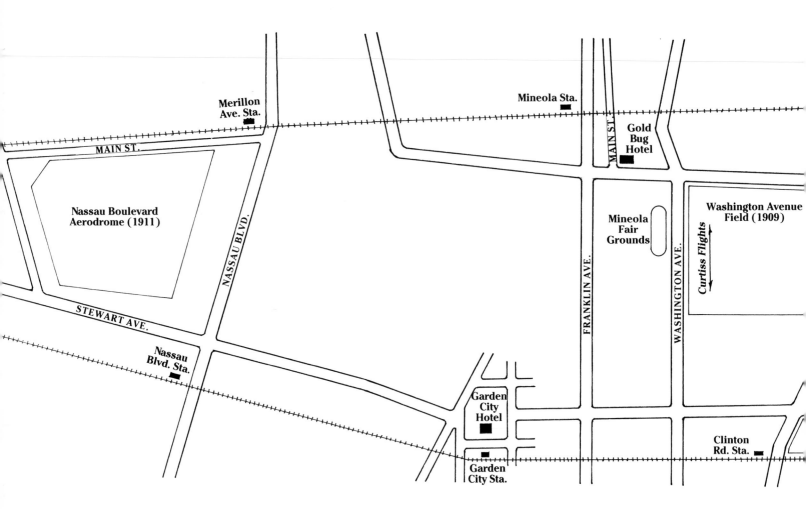

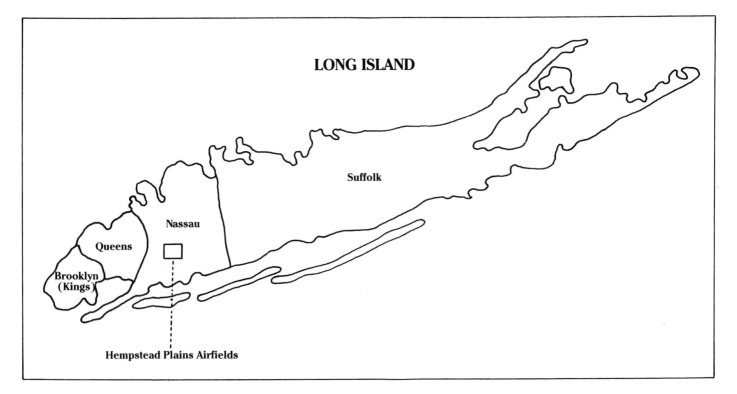

COMPOSITE MAP, 1909–PRESENT

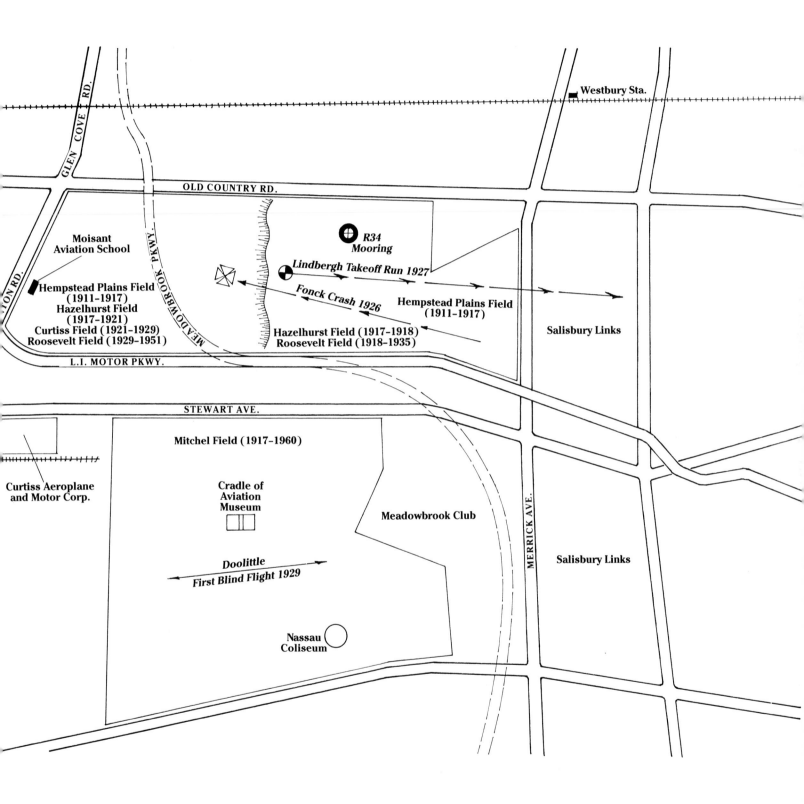

Hempstead Plains Airfields: Composite Map, 1909–present.
(*Map drawn by and reproduced through the courtesy of Russ Moore.*)
(*Inset:* Long Island, Showing Hempstead Plains Airfields.)

1. After the Wright brothers' triumph at Kitty Hawk in December 1903, progress with flying machines in the United States, apart from the Wrights' further work, was surprisingly slow. Not until March 1908 did anyone else make a flight (F. W. "Casey" Baldwin in an Aerial Experiment Association biplane at Hammondsport, New York). The inaugural heavier-than-air flight on Long Island came soon thereafter; it was made, ironically, by a Frenchman of English extraction, Henri Farman (1874–1934). Farman, a great aviator much honored by the French in later years, flew his machine (seen here), a modified Voisin biplane, about 400 yards on July 31, 1908, at the Brighton Beach Race Track in Brooklyn, before members and friends of the Aero Club of America. During the following week Farman made several other exhibition flights, becoming thereby the first foreigner to fly in America, as well as the first of a long and distinguished line of Long Island aviators. In a way he could not know then, Farman directly inspired at least one future leading light of Long Island aviation, Lawrence Sperry, then not quite sixteen, who rode to Brighton Beach from Flatbush by motorcycle before the crack of dawn to witness one of Farman's flights. *(Photo by A. Radcliffe Dugmore; Frank Strnad Collection.)*

2–4. The history of lighter-than-air flight on Long Island goes back to June 15, 1833, when Prof. Charles F. Durant ascended in a balloon from Castle Garden, New York (on Manhattan Island), and touched down at the Union Course racetrack in Woodhaven, Long Island (now part of the borough of Queens, New York City). Long Island never became a great center of balloon or dirigible flight, but it had its notable events. Lincoln Beachey (1887–1915) was a pioneering stunt flier who, before he became interested in airplanes, flew airships throughout the United States. He demonstrated his famous one-man airship, the *Rubber Cow* (seen here), at Jamaica Oval Ball Field, 89th and Jamaica Avenues, Jamaica, Queens, in 1908. *(Photos by Frederick T. Weber; courtesy of The Queens Borough Public Library.)*
5. The race to conquer the air was not won haphazardly. Experimenters worked constantly to find the best wing shapes, the best engines, the best propellers. Sometimes the experiments were fun—at least Joe Post seems to be enjoying himself here as he tests a propeller on a "fan-cycle," a special bicycle built by Henry and Will Newell for that very purpose. Richmond Hill, Queens, August 1909. *(Photo by Will Newell; Nassau County Museum Reference Library.)*

6

6. Early aviators emerged from many backgrounds; many were mechanics or military men. The honor of being the first flying dentist belonged to Dr. Henry W. Walden of Long Island. His most notable achievement involved his monoplane at Mineola, beginning late in 1909. Earlier, he exhibited a biplane at the Morris Park Race Track in the Bronx, 1909, shown here. (*National Air and Space Museum, Washington, D.C.*)

7. The great Glenn Curtiss (1878–1930) of Hammondsport, New York, exerted a major influence on aircraft design and construction in the United States for many years. His *Golden Flyer* biplane broke records in early days. Curtiss sold one in June 1909 to the Aeronautic Society of New York, shown here at the Morris Park Race Track in the Bronx. This marked the first commercial sale of an aircraft in the United States. Curtiss moved to Long Island the following month, and soon he and his *Golden Flyer* and other planes were to make an enormous impact on Long Island flying. (*Nassau County Museum Reference Library.*)

7

9

8

8, 9. Glenn Curtiss *(photo 8)* was a motorcycle racer who designed and built his own engines. Following the Wrights' success in 1903, Curtiss joined a group of men under the leadership of Dr. Alexander Graham Bell, the famous inventor, to form the Aerial Experiment Association, which began experimenting with flying machines late in 1907. Curtiss participated in the designing of many of the Association's airplanes, the first of which was flown at Hammondsport in upstate New York on March 12, 1908. On July 4, 1909, flying the *June Bug,* the first plane primarily of his own design, Curtiss won the *Scientific American* prize for the first public flight of one kilometer in a straight line. Eventually Curtiss' design for ailerons was to replace the Wrights' "wing warping" as the standard device for banking an airplane in a turn.

On July 10, 1909, Curtiss shifted the base of his flying operations to Long Island, establishing the Hempstead Plains near Mineola as a center of aviation for many years to come. A vast, flat, sparsely populated meadow, the Hempstead Plains were an aviator's dream. In succeeding years, innumerable records were to be set and broken and some of the world's most outstanding feats of flight accomplished at Hazelhurst Field, Curtiss Field, Roosevelt Field, and Mitchel Field—all names of different areas (or the same areas at different times) into which this part of the Hempstead Plains was divided at various periods.

The first of these achievements was Glenn Curtiss' own flight at the Washington Avenue field adjoining the Mineola Fair Grounds (actually in Garden City, just to the west of the area about to develop into the major flying fields), on July 17, 1909. A crowd of 2,500 watched as he circled the field in his *Golden Flyer* biplane for 52 minutes, 30 seconds *(photo 9),* earning him the *Scientific American* prize for the second consecutive year—an award of $10,000 for a flight of over 25 kilometers (his actual distance was nearly 25 *miles*). All this was only the beginning of Curtiss' distinguished career as an aviator, flying instructor, and particularly designer and builder of pioneering airplanes, ending abruptly with his untimely death in 1930. *(Photo 8: Garden City [N.Y.] Archives; photo 9 by Joseph Burt; Cradle of Aviation Museum, Mitchel Field, N.Y.)*

11

12

10. Glenn Curtiss trained a whole school of aviators, of whom Charles F. Willard became the first to follow him in piloting the *Golden Flyer* successfully. Not all of Curtiss' students, however, were so quick to master the technique of flying, as is evident here in the inverted position of the *Golden Flyer*, August 3, 1909, ten minutes after Alexander Williams' attempt at flight (Washington Avenue field). *(Courtesy of The Queens Borough Public Library.)*

11, 12. The first outstanding aeronautical feat in a monoplane was the Frenchman Louis Blériot's famous flight across the English Channel on July 25, 1909. Following this achievement, Dr. Henry W. Walden, the flying dentist, was the first American to design and build a successful monoplane, shown here at the Washington Avenue field in Garden City (fall 1909) where it was to exceed a speed of fifty miles an hour in test flights in December 1909. *(National Air and Space Museum.)*

13. This sleepy, quaint country inn, Peter Mc-Laughlin's Gold Bug Hotel (Old Country Road, Mineola, winter 1909–10) was selected for a major role in Long Island aviation history when Glenn Curtiss made it his Long Island headquarters. The owner was quick to capitalize on its potential: note the sign proclaiming the hotel "Aeronautical Headquarters." McLaughlin, standing in the center in the photograph, was already involved in aviation (see photo 28) and evidently had Curtiss' plane the *Golden Flyer* (nicknamed "Gold Bug" after an earlier plane, the *June Bug*) in mind when naming his hotel. *(Nassau County Museum Reference Library and George C. Dade Collection.)*

14. A tent adjacent to the hotel served as a hangar. Here Curtiss (second from right) is standing with his associates in front of his famous *Golden Flyer*, August 12, 1909. Standing at the left before the plane is Charles F. Willard, one of Curtiss' principal pilots. *(Nassau County Museum Reference Library.)*

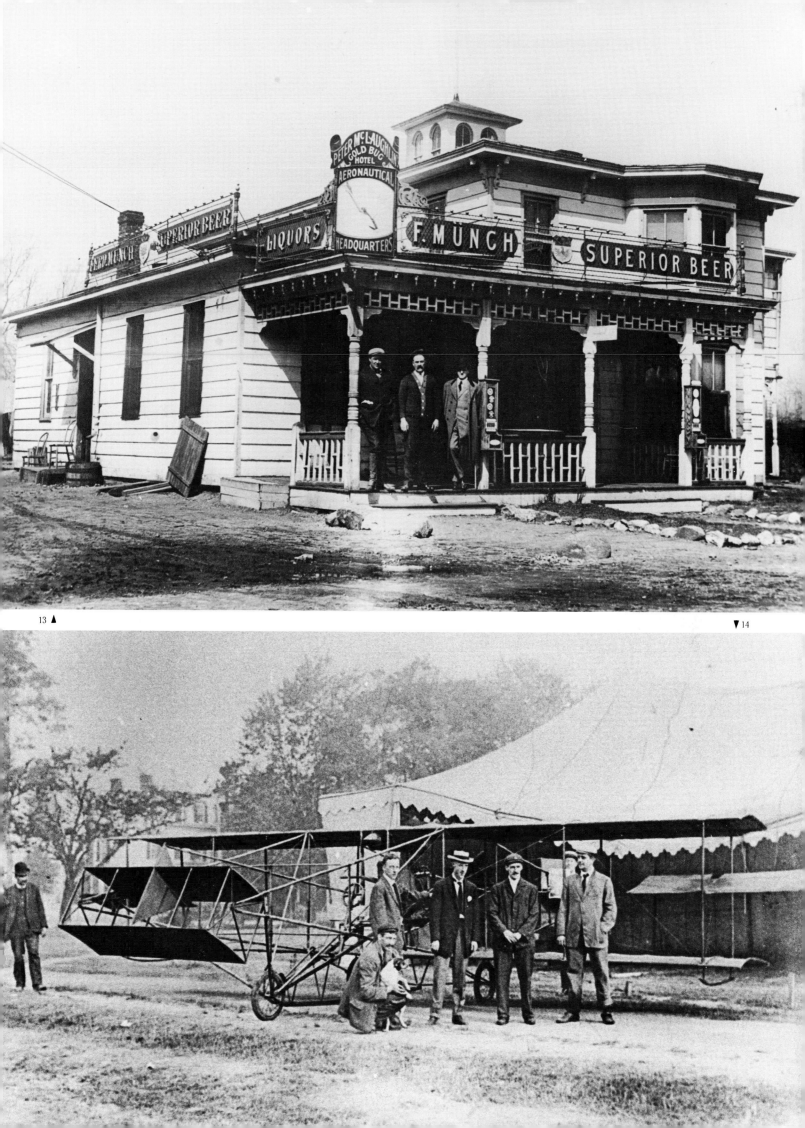

13 ▲

▼ 14

15

16

15, 16. Clifford B. Harmon (1869–1945), a wealthy aviation enthusiast and, earlier, a distinguished balloonist, was the first to fly a plane across Long Island Sound, traveling from Mineola (actually Garden City) to Greenwich, Connecticut. He is seen here at the Washington Avenue field in his Farman biplane (purchased from Claude Grahame-White) before *(photo 15)* and just after *(photo 16)* takeoff. Harmon won the "Country Life in America" trophy for the feat, accomplished on August 20, 1910. *(Photo 15 by Fred Weber; courtesy of The Queens Borough Public Library. Photo 16: Garden City Archives.)*

17

17–26. The third international air tournament in America was held, fittingly enough, on Long Island. The spectators at Belmont Park Race Track—a still popular horse-racing track located just across the New York City line in Nassau County—included prominent social figures, among them Lt.-Gov. Timothy L. Woodruff. The possibilities of aviation as a competitive sport, with the exciting challenges that the new flying machines might overcome, were beginning to gain widespread attention. The International Aviation Tournament occupied nine days in October 1910, from the 22nd to the 30th. "Birdmen" from England and France competed with American fliers for three major prizes (among various lesser awards). The Gordon Bennett race (for speed)—with a $5,000 cash prize—was won by Claude Grahame-White of England (Alfred Leblanc, a Frenchman, had reached a higher speed—nearly 70 mph—but was disqualified by

crashing at the end). Grahame-White also captured the Thomas Fortune Ryan prize of $10,000 for winning a round-trip race to the Statue of Liberty (it took two years for this race to be decided; John B. Moisant, an American contestant, was eventually disqualified for starting late, although his flying time had been slightly better than Grahame-White's).

Two daredevil Americans were the final competitors for the $5,000 altitude prize. Ralph Johnstone and Arch Hoxsey (both flying Wright biplanes), who had been among the first pilots trained by Orville Wright, both soared further and further into the blue until they ran out of fuel and glided down to safety in fields many miles from Belmont Park. (The two became known jocularly as "The Heavenly Twins.") When Johnstone captured the prize he also set a world altitude record of 9,714 feet.

The excitement of such a competition at that

time—barely seven years after the Wright brothers had first met the challenge of sustained, controlled heavier-than-air flight—can scarcely be imagined today. Planes built by the Wrights and by Glenn Curtiss were entered in the contests, although none of these men were themselves contestants. Both biplanes and monoplanes (some built by Blériot, the famous French aviator) of what would soon seem primitive designs raced around the pylons and across land and water in this spectacular American flying tournament. Despite the dangers of competitive flying, miraculously no one was killed (though more than one plane was wrecked) at the Belmont tournament. (Nevertheless both Johnstone and Hoxsey, as well as John B. Moisant, died in flying accidents later in 1910.) *17:* Claude Grahame-White in his Blériot XI (no. 10).

18: Radley in his Blériot XI (no. 23), flying past the pylon and scoreboard. *19:* The monoplane at the top is Hubert Latham's Antoinette (no. 1), flying over the grandstand. *20:* Grahame-White flying a Farman biplane (no. 10). *21:* A closer view of the scoreboard. The letters in the left-hand column ("KO" under "AB") indicate a wind of 10 to 15 mph. The figures under "BC" and "CD" show that pilot number 16 has completed 9 laps of the 2,500-meter course and that pilot number 21 has completed 6 laps. *22:* Émile Aubrun in an Antoinette monoplane (no. 1), with a Wright biplane in the background. *23:* The wreckage of Clifford B. Harmon's Farman biplane, after John B. Moisant had taxied his Blériot monoplane into it. *24:* Roland Garros in his Demoiselle (no. 9).

23

24

25

27

25: A special monoplane version of the Curtiss biplane, built for Curtiss exhibition flier Eugene B. Ely (1886–1911). *26:* The biplane of John A. D. McCurdy (the first man to have flown an airplane in Canada) after a crack-up. The man with the mustache and derby in the center of the photograph may possibly be Orville Wright, who attended but did not compete in the Tournament. *(Photo 17: George C. Dade Collection. Photos 18 and 22 by Edwin Levick; National Air and Space Museum. Other photos: Nassau County Museum Reference Library.)*
27. Earle Ovington (1879–1936), later to win fame as the first official airmail pilot, is seen here landing his Blériot *Dragon-Fly* at Belmont Park (date uncertain, but very possibly during the International Aviation Tournament, October 22–30, 1910). *(Photo by Joseph Burt; John Drennan Collection.)*

28, 29. With the appearance of posters like this *(photo 28)*, aeronautics as popular entertainment may be said to have come of age. Daredevil exhibition flying would soon spread across the nation, Tod Shriver being only one of many stunt pilots. Capt. Thomas Scott Baldwin (1864–1923) was a famous American dirigible balloonist (airship pilot). By 1908, a dirigible designed by Baldwin had been purchased by the Aeronautical Division of the U.S. Army Signal Corps. Baldwin did not begin flying an airplane until 1910, a Curtiss-type biplane painted a bright red, which he named the *Red Devil*, shown standing at the Washington Avenue field, Garden City, 1910 *(photo 29)*. P. F. McLaughlin *(photo 28)* was also the owner of the Gold Bug Hotel (see above, photo 13). *(Photo 28 by Joseph Burt; courtesy of The Queens Borough Public Library. Photo 29 by Henry Otto Korten; Nassau County Museum Reference Library.)*

30. St. Croix Johnstone poses for the camera in his Moisant-Blériot monoplane at the Hempstead Plains field, Mineola, June 22, 1911. On July 27 Johnstone established an American speed record in this plane at the same location. *(Photo by Joseph Burt; John Drennan Collection.)*

31. This first successful two-seat Blériot-type monoplane flown in the United States was built by the American Aeroplane Supply House, Hempstead, New York. Shown are pilot Willie Haupt and passenger George McNamara at the Washington Avenue field, July 1911. At the right may be seen the stables of the Mineola Fair Grounds. *(Nassau County Museum Reference Library.)*

30

31

32

32. A. L. Welsh, one of the first Wright-trained pilots, flies his Wright biplane over the flat expanse of the Hempstead Plains field (late summer or early fall 1911), Mineola. Also known as the Hempstead Plains Aerodrome, this field included at that time the whole area to the east of Clinton Road, Garden City. Much later this field would be divided into Curtiss and Roosevelt Fields. The reason why Glenn Curtiss and others chose this site is made immediately clear by this photograph. *(Photo by Joseph Burt; John Drennan Collection.)*

33–35. On September 17, 1911, the Sheepshead Bay Speedway, Brooklyn, was the starting point of the first transcontinental flight—that of Cal Rodgers *(photo 33)* in a Wright model "EX" biplane (shown, *photos 34 and 35*, being assembled at the starting point). Calbraith Perry Rodgers (1879–1912) was a former college football player and cousin of the famous Navy pilot John Rodgers. In 1911, Cal, adventurous and more than a little reckless, persuaded the Armour meat-packing company to sponsor his attempt to win the Hearst prize, the famous newspaper entrepreneur's offer of $50,000 to the first person to fly from coast to coast within thirty days. The name of Armour's new soft drink, "Vin Fiz," became the name of Rodgers' plane, and a special railroad train was engaged to follow him carrying members of his family, his manager, three mechanics (including the expert Charlie Taylor, who had worked with the Wright brothers on the first airplanes), an automobile and chauf-

feur, and more than enough spare parts for the *Vin Fiz* to build a complete second plane.

The flight, never much exceeding 50 mph, proceeded via Chicago, Kansas City, and the Southwest to avoid the Rocky Mountains. It turned into a series of mishaps. Rodgers got lost, had his plane damaged by thoughtless fans, had engine trouble and other mechanical problems, crashed a number of times and was badly injured, and made some 65 forced landings in all. Yet there was excitement in Rodgers' path and he persisted to surmount every obstacle. On November 5, 49 days after he had departed from Sheepshead Bay, Rodgers landed in Pasadena, California. (Actual flying time for the 4,231-mile zigzag course to Pasadena was 82 hours, 4 minutes, averaging about 52 mph.) Too late to win the Hearst prize, he had still become the first person to span the continent by air, and for this feat he was awarded a gold medal by the Aero Club of America. Still dissatisfied, on November 12, Rodgers set out to dip his plane's wheels in the surf of the Pacific Ocean. After being delayed a month by another serious accident in which he was knocked unconscious, he finally made it to the ocean at Long Beach on December 10. By this time, the *Vin Fiz* had been almost entirely rebuilt and Rodgers needed crutches to walk. Five months later he was dead, killed in a bizarre flying accident near Long Beach. *(Photo 33: Frank Strnad Collection; photos 34 and 35: Nassau County Museum Reference Library.)*

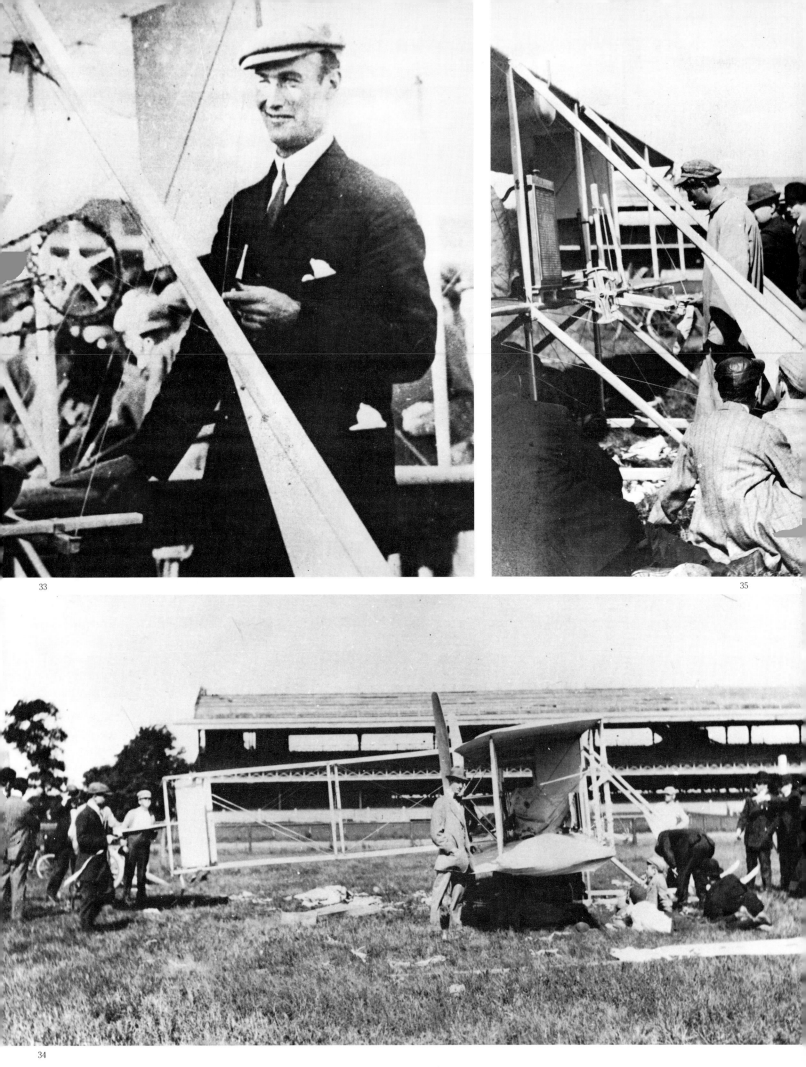

33

35

34

36–38. Another International Aviation Meet was held on Long Island from September 23 to 30, 1911. This time the site was the Nassau Boulevard Aerodrome in Garden City, to the west of the Washington Avenue field. Aviation had by this time gathered a band of its own celebrities. Naturally many were to be seen at this tournament, including (*photo 37,* left to right) Capt. Thomas S. Baldwin, James C. ("Bud") Mars, and Eugene B. Ely. Ely, one of Glenn Curtiss' pilots, had recently made history as the first man to take off in an airplane from the deck of a ship (the battleship U.S.S. *Birmingham,* on November 14, 1910) and to land an airplane on the deck of a ship (the cruiser U.S.S. *Pennsylvania,* January 18, 1911). *Photo 38* shows Capt. Baldwin's Curtiss-type biplane. *(Photo 36: Nassau County Museum Reference Library. Photo 37 by Henry I. Newell; Nassau County Museum Reference Library. Photo 38 by Henry I. Newell.)*

39

39. Two Wright biplanes circle over the Nassau
Boulevard Aerodrome, Garden City, 1911. *(Photo
by Joseph Burt; John Drennan Collection.)*
40. The first U.S. woman to solo in a heavier-
than-air flying machine was Blanche Stuart
Scott (1886–1970), here seen taking off in a
Curtiss pusher biplane, Washington Avenue
field, Garden City, July 27, 1911. *(Nassau
County Museum Reference Library.)*
41. Blanche Stuart Scott. *(Walter Winicki
Collection.)*

[21]

44

45

42, 43. Frederick Hild in the cockpit *(photo 42)* of his American-built Blériot-type monoplane (and, in *photo 43,* standing in front of it), summer 1911. The manufacturer, the American Aeroplane Supply House, also operated a school on the site of these photographs, the Hempstead Plains aviation field (note the sign in the Hild and Marshonet hangar). *(Photos by Joseph Burt; John Drennan Collection.)*

44, 45. The first official delivery of mail by airplane in the United States took place at the beginning of the 1911 International Aviation Meet,

on September 23. More precisely, this historical "first" occurred when Earle Ovington received a bag of mail from A. H. Bartsch of the Bosch Magneto Company *(photo 44)* and carried it in his 70-hp Blériot *Dragon-Fly* from the Nassau Boulevard Aerodrome to a prearranged spot in Mineola, about three miles away, where he dropped it for waiting postal officials to claim. The bag broke on contact with the ground, scattering its contents of 640 letters and 1,280 postcards, but the mail was all retrieved and delivered. A sturdier bag was used on succeeding

days of the Aviation Meet, when the airmail operation was successfully repeated a number of times. *(Photo 44: National Air and Space Museum. Photo 45: Frank Strnad Collection.)*

46. Contrary to widespread belief, this photograph does *not* depict the first airmail dispatch. The plane and pilot are the same, but the other man is U.S. Postmaster General Frank H. Hitchcock, and the date is two days later, September 25, 1911. *(Nassau County Museum Reference Library.)*

46

47–51. Before the Wright brothers applied to flying the true principles of aerodynamics, would-be fliers entertained all sorts of fanciful notions about what was necessary to imitate the birds and soar through the air. The pre-Wright mentality persisted even after their success, and a few of the resulting bizarre airplanes were made, tested, and flown—if they could fly at all—on Long Island. The Geary Circular Triplane (*photo 47*, August 17, 1911) needless to say was not successful. Experimenter Howard Huntington developed aircraft such as that seen here near his house in Hollis, Queens, January 22, 1914 (*photo 48*). His more modest *Clam* made successful flights on the Hempstead Plains field (seen here on its second flight, June 20, 1914; *photo 49*).

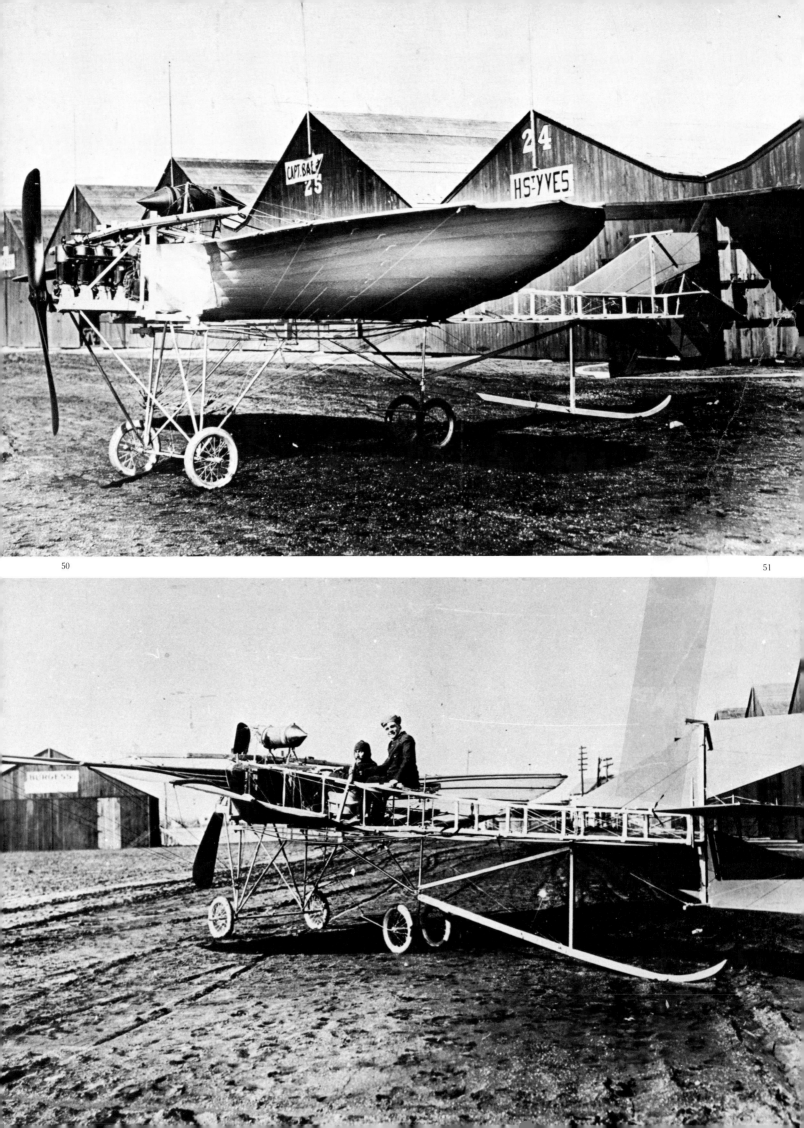

The Fity monoplane (Nassau Boulevard Aerodrome, fall 1911) had folding wings for easy storage *(photos 50 and 51)*, a practical idea that later found its way into the design of many aircraft. *(Photos 47–49 courtesy of The Queens Borough Public Library. Photos 50 and 51: Nassau County Museum Reference Library.)*
52, 53. Women quickly followed men into the air. Harriet Quimby (1884–1912), a drama critic, became on August 1, 1911, the first American woman to be licensed as a pilot (and the second woman in the world to be so licensed). She was the thirty-seventh licensed pilot of the Aero Club of America, as well as the only woman in the U.S. to operate a monoplane. Miss Quimby is shown here at the Hempstead Plains field in her Moisant monoplane on the occasion of a flight to the Nassau Boulevard Aerodrome *(photo 52)*. (In *photo 53* her passenger is Shakir S. Jerwan, instructor at the Moisant Aviation School, where she trained; same location, June 1912.) Miss Quimby's end was as tragically abrupt as those of many male colleagues: shortly after these photographs were taken she was killed in an air accident at Boston Harbor. *(Photo 52: National Air and Space Museum. Photo 53 by Joseph Burt; John Drennan Collection.)*

54

55

56

54, 55. The development of seaplanes followed closely that of land airplanes. At a time when there were few airfields on land, seaplanes had the advantage of being able to land wherever there was sufficient water. On Long Island, flying "hydroaeroplanes"—Wright biplanes equipped with pontoons—was taught at the Wright Hydro-aeroplane School, operated by Charles Wald. Two views of planes are seen here near the school, 1912, at the Glenwood Country Club, Glen Head, in Nassau County on Hempstead Bay (opening into Long Island Sound). Wald was heralded as the first "air ferryman" when he carried a bag of mail across the Sound to New Rochelle in Westchester County on September 21, 1912, the first flight across the Sound in a seaplane. *(Photo 54: Walter Jankowski Collection. Photo 55: Carl "Slim" Hennicke Collection.)*

56. A Sunday afternoon in 1913 at Hempstead Plains shows an interesting lineup of mono-planes: (from left to right) a Heinrich, two Sloane-Deperdussins, and a Moisant. *(Photo by Henry S. Villard.)*

57. Lincoln Beachey, the great stunt and exhibition flier (and former dirigible pilot; see photos 2–4), flew his Curtiss biplanes around the country. On May 23, 1914, he raced Barney Oldfield (in racer, bottom left) at the Brighton Beach Race Track, Brooklyn. *(National Air and Space Museum.)*
58. The Heinrich brothers of Baldwin designed and built the first American monoplane powered by an American engine, as well as a number of other successful monoplanes and biplanes. Here Arthur Heinrich is shown with Mrs. Mary Sims in a two-seat Heinrich monoplane, Hempstead Plains, June 20, 1914. *(Nassau County Museum Reference Library.)*
59, 60. Lawrence Sperry (1892–1923) was a son of the famous inventor Elmer A. Sperry, and with his father developed many revolutionary instruments and devices for airplanes. Perhaps the most important was the gyro-stabilizer—the first automatic pilot. This was installed in a Curtiss "F" flying boat and won a 50,000-franc prize from the French government in a spectacular demonstration in a competition at Bezons, France, July 3, 1914. In *photo 60,* Sperry's mechanic stands on a wing to demonstrate a function of this gyro-stabilizer. Sperry later set up operations on Long Island, where he was a major figure in aviation there until his untimely death in 1923.

The gyro-stabilizer is one of those inventions the importance of which cannot be overestimated. Before, pilots had to operate the controls continually to keep their planes steady in shifting winds; with the automatic pilot in use, their attention was freed. They could tend to the exigencies of weather or warfare, watch for beacons on land or obstacles in the air, or simply relax. Few of the significant achievements in aviation in later years would have been possible without this device. *(Both photos: Thomas Foxworth Collection.)*

61. Not all the flying activity on the Hempstead Plains field was limited to full-size airplanes. Model-plane racing already attracted many enthusiasts. The Henry S. Villard Model Aeroplane Trophy and cash prizes were awarded at the First National Model Aeroplane Competition, August 22, 1915. *(Photo by Henry S. Villard.)*

62. By 1915 the First World War was already raging in Europe, and much thought was given to the military uses of airplanes. In this year, Albert S. Heinrich demonstrated to the Italian government the plane shown here at the Hempstead Plains field, the Heinrich Tractor Biplane, featuring a powerful 100-hp gyro engine. The Heinrich company's hangar in the photograph is the former Moisant Flying School hangar. The letter "M" (of "Moisant") can be discerned between the words "Heinrich" and "Aeroplane." *(Nassau County Museum Reference Library.)*

62

63

64

65

63, 64. Since Long Island in the teens was a center of both aviation and the film industry, it was only natural that airplanes and flying should make their way onto the silver screen. Pearl White, silent-movie star, and other members of the cast of *Pearl of the Army* are seen here on the Hempstead Plains field during filming in the winter of 1915–16. *(Both photos courtesy of The Queens Borough Public Library.)*
65. The Curtiss "F" flying boat was to be involved in much significant flying activity—especially that of the U.S. Navy—in the next few years. The one shown here (summer 1916) was used by the new First Battalion of the Naval Militia of the State of New York at Bay Shore on the Great South Bay, Suffolk County. With the ever-present possibility of American involvement in the war, it was thought advisable to train a national corps of volunteers for naval aviation work. *(Northport Historical Society.)*

66, 67. At the same time, also in the summer of 1916, a group of civilians under the leadership of F. Trubee Davison formed the first Yale Unit, Aerial Coast Patrol Unit Number 1, at Huntington on Suffolk County's north shore. This group of 29 aviators was offered by Mr. Davison to the Navy in the event of war. Soon it formed the nucleus of the First Naval Reserve Flying Corps, the basis of the Foreign Service of the U.S. Naval Aviation Force. Their first plane of choice was, again, the Curtiss "F," seen here being tested on Long Island Sound at Huntington Beach. *(Both photos: Kenneth Smith Collection.)*

68, 69. Glenn Curtiss' planes were also widely used by the Army. The ten JN-4's—the famous Curtiss "Jenny"—in *photo 68,* taken at Mineola, November 18, 1916, were flown in the first mass cross-country flight in U.S. military aviation history. The ten planes, belonging to the New York National Guard's First Aero Company *(photo 69),* were flown together to Princeton, New Jersey, on the 18th and returned to Mineola the following day. *(Both photos courtesy of The Queens Borough Public Library.)*

70, 71. Although rockets were used against German observation balloons by Allied pursuit planes in World War I, it is unusual to see rockets being tested on a Curtiss Jenny trainer (Mineola, March 1917). *(Both photos courtesy of The Queens Borough Public Library.)*

71

72. On May 3, 1917, the Hempstead Plains Aerodrome, Mineola (actually unincorporated Nassau County east of Garden City, but traditionally called "Mineola"), became Hazelhurst Field, after Lt. Leighton W. Hazelhurst, distinguished Army aviator. This photograph of a lineup of Curtiss Jennies, taken that spring, looks toward Old Country Road, the airfield's northern boundary. *(Nassau County Museum Reference Library.)*

73. Military air-training activities often led to wrecked planes, like this Jenny (Mineola, spring 1917). The Curtiss JN-4 was by far the most popular trainer aircraft. *(Courtesy of The Queens Borough Public Library.)*

74. In July 1917, Hangar No. 8 on the west side of Hazelhurst Field was converted into a supply depot, and a tower was mounted on the roof. This was the first use of a control tower on a Long Island airfield. The tower operator had no control over the aircraft; he was up there to watch for crashes, blow the siren, and direct the crash crew. *(Nassau County Museum Reference Library.)*

75. The first factory on Long Island that was built specifically for the construction of aircraft was the L. W. F. Engineering Corporation building in College Point, Queens, on Flushing Bay, shown here shortly after its completion in 1917. *(National Air and Space Museum.)*

76. The interior of the L. W. F. building, showing the three-engined "Owl," at that time the largest U.S.-built land aircraft, under construction. *(National Air and Space Museum.)*

77. A view of Hazelhurst Field in 1918, at the end of World War I. These hangars, built by the Army Air Service in 1917, survived until 1956, when they were torn down to make way for the Roosevelt Field Shopping Center. (*U.S. Air Force Museum, Dayton, Ohio.*)

78. Belmont Park continued to be the site of many a spectacular flying event. Here Lt. Meany of the U.S. Air Service, flying a Thomas-Morse S-4C "Scout," races Louis Chevrolet (in the racing car below) in a military show on April 6,

1918. (*Nassau County Museum Reference Library.*)

79. The reliable Curtiss JN-4H "Jenny" once again figured in air history on May 15, 1918, when the first successful scheduled U.S. Air Mail Service flight was made by Lt. Torrey Webb. Lt. Webb is shown here with his wife and an army officer at the New York Air Mail Terminal at Belmont Park (in Elmont, N.Y., just over the New York City line) before his takeoff for Philadelphia with 150 pounds of mail. In Philadel-

phia, Webb conveyed the mail to Lt. James Clark Edgerton, who flew it to Washington, its ultimate destination, on time. (Total elapsed time was 3 hours, 20 minutes.) A similar airmail flight was supposed to have taken place simultaneously in the opposite direction, but a series of mishaps set this part of the operation back a day. The entire operation was directed by Maj. R. H. Fleet. (*Nassau County Museum Reference Library.*)

80. Quentin Roosevelt, the youngest son of President Theodore Roosevelt, was one of the more distinguished Long Islanders, having been born in Oyster Bay in 1897. One of the first pilots trained at Hazelhurst Field, Roosevelt showed great promise as a military pilot but met an untimely end when he was shot down in action over France on July 14, 1918. It was in his honor that the name of the eastern section of Hazelhurst Field was changed to Roosevelt Field on September 24, 1918. *(Nassau County Museum Reference Library.)*

81. During the war the U.S. Navy took over operation of the Bay Shore Air Station, expanding the facilities built by the state Naval Militia in 1916. Over a thousand men were trained there as seaplane pilots and mechanics. From April 15, 1918, to December 1, 1918 (the period of this photograph), 18,862 hours of flying time were logged, an impressive record considering that at no time were there more than 64 aircraft at the station. *(George Haddad Collection.)*

82. Before the Hindenburg disaster in 1937, dirigibles were still considered a viable means of air transportation. About six miles west of Montauk Point—the extreme eastern tip of Long Island, about 120 miles east of New York City—on a strip of land between Fort Pond and the Atlantic Ocean, the Navy maintained an air station that included a dirigible hangar, shown here. Patrols of both dirigibles and seaplanes were put in operation beginning October 20, 1917. The patrols covered a considerable range, all the way from Fire Island Light, about 75 miles to the west of this air station, to Nantucket Shoals, Massachusetts, about as far to the east. The first commander of the Montauk Naval Air Station was Lt. Marc A. Mitscher, who later, as Adm. Mitscher, was celebrated for his activities in the Pacific in World War II. *(George Haddad Collection.)*

81

83. To all appearances this is an ordinary bi-plane of the period around World War I. Actually it is far more remarkable: the world's first air guided missile. Built jointly by the Curtiss and Sperry companies, the "Aerial Torpedo," as it was known, featured a Sperry gyro-stabilizer. This automatic pilot enabled it to fly, laden with explosives, without a human pilot on board. Many successful test flights were made in 1918 from a secret airfield on the edge of Great South Bay near Amityville. The war ended, however, before the "Aerial Torpedo" could be used. (*Gary Fisk Collection.*)

84–86. The New York City Police Department Aerial Police Squadron was formed in April 1919, under the leadership of Col. Jefferson de Mont Thompson, at the Sheepshead Bay Speedway in Brooklyn. Many well-known aviators were members, some of them having flown in the war against Germany. *84:* An assembly of air police ready for flight in front of one of their planes at Sheepshead Bay. *85:* Rosaline Dwyer, daughter of police Inspector John F. Dwyer, and the squad's mascot, hands a letter to a flying policeman. *86:* An Aerial Squadron plane—a Curtiss Jenny—in a practice flight at Sheeps-head Bay. (*All photos: Frank Strnad Collection.*)

84

85

86

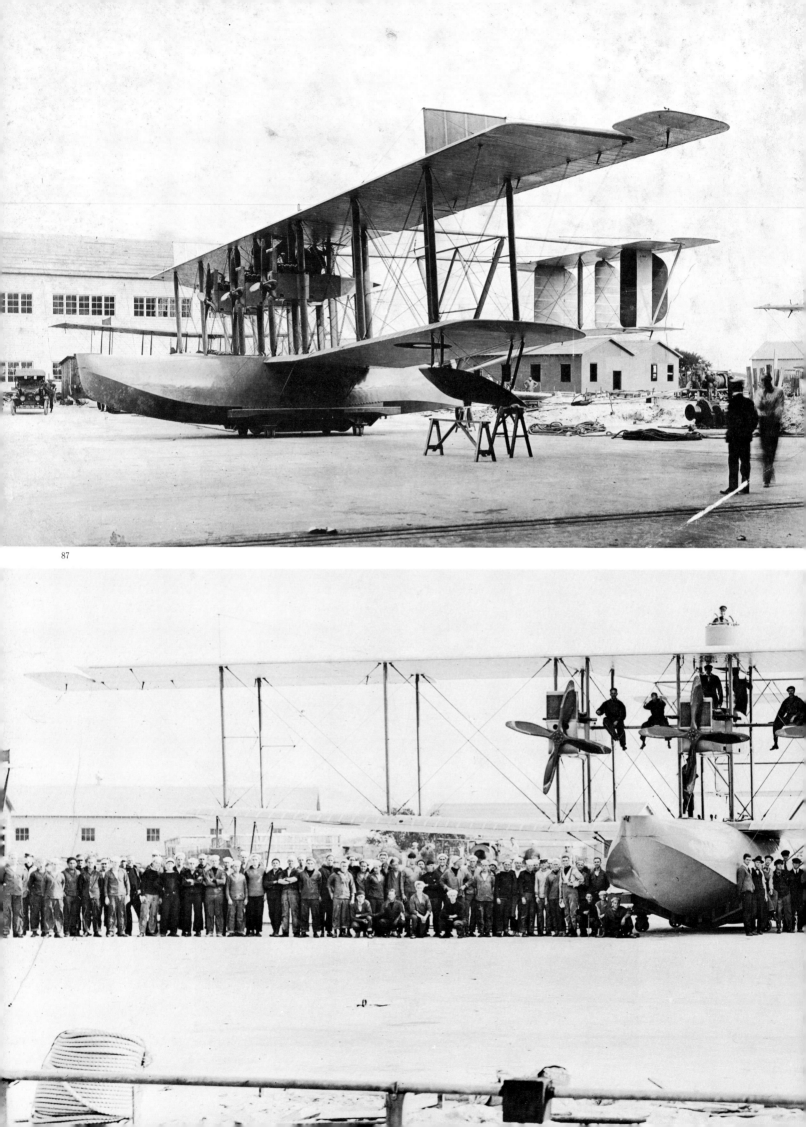

87–93. The capabilities of heavier-than-air flying machines became increasingly evident during the First World War; after the war the great challenge to aviators was the crossing of the Atlantic Ocean. Technology did not yet permit direct flights between New York and London or Paris, but it was thought that the distance between Newfoundland and Ireland or Portugal via the Azores, about 2,000 miles, might be spanned. The first successful crossing of this type was a carefully planned operation of the U.S. Navy using three Curtiss seaplanes built at the Garden City plant: the *NC-1, NC-3,* and *NC-4* (the *NC-2,* damaged by fire, was scrapped to provide parts for the other planes).

These planes were very large for their day (wingspan 126 feet, length 68 feet) and very powerful, each with four engines totaling 1,600 hp and tanks holding almost 2,000 gallons of fuel. (*Photo 87* shows the *NC-1* at Far Rockaway, some months before the flight.) Of course, as hydroaeroplanes, these aircraft could float on the water, but, as a further safeguard

against disaster, the Navy sent out a fleet of several dozen cruisers and destroyers to cover the route between Newfoundland and the first stop, the Azores, so that if necessary the crew of a disabled plane could be rescued.

The three planes took off from Jamaica Bay at Far Rockaway, Queens, on May 8, 1919 (*photo 91* shows the *NC-4* aloft, location uncertain). After a stop at Halifax, Nova Scotia (Chatham, Massachusetts, and then Cape Cod for the *NC-4*) the planes proceeded to Trepassey Bay, Newfoundland, where the oceanic crossing began on May 16. The *NC-1* (commanded by Lt.-Comdr. P. N. L. Bellinger) lost its way over the Atlantic and ultimately sank; its crew was rescued by a passing steamer. The *NC-3* (led by the fleet commander, Comdr. J. H. Towers) eventually made it to Ponta Delgada, on São Miguel Island in the Azores, but only after taxiing on the water for the final 200 miles. But the *NC-4,* under the leadership of Lt.-Comdr. A. C. Read and piloted by Lt. Walter Hinton, reached Horta on the island of Faial in the Azores midday

(1:33 P.M., Greenwich time) on May 17. Flying time from Trepassey Bay to Horta was 15 hours, 18 minutes. The *NC-4* alone proceeded to the continent, arriving in Lisbon on May 27, having flown nonstop from Ponta Delgada in 9 hours, 43 minutes. The total distance covered from Trepassey Bay to Lisbon was 2,400 miles. The *NC-4* continued from Lisbon to Plymouth, England, arriving May 31, and was returned to the United States by ship and placed on triumphal display in New York's Central Park from July 14 through July 28, 1919. (The *NC-4* is now on permanent display at the Naval Aviation Museum, Pensacola, Florida.) The oceanic barrier between the Old World and the New had been bridged by air for the first time. *87:* The *NC-1* at Far Rockaway, shortly after its construction (October 3, 1918). *88:* The *NC-1* before takeoff, Far Rockaway. The string of people under the wings dramatizes the enormous wingspan of these planes.

89: Lt. Hinton adjusts the compass of the *NC-3.*
Lt.-Comdr. R. E. Byrd looks on (Byrd assisted in
flight preparation though he did not participate
in the actual venture). *90:* The *NC-4* at its mooring, Far Rockaway. *91:* The *NC-4* in the air.

92: The *NC-4* off Lisbon, May 28, 1919. *93:* The
NC-4 on display in Central Park, New York, July
1919. *(Photo 87–89, 91, and 92: Hayward Cirker
Collection. Photo 90: Roger Seybel Collection.
Photo 93: Frank Strnad Collection.)*

94

94–97. In 1919, the trans-Atlantic crossing of an
airship was an event almost as notable as that
of an airplane. The first successful such crossing was completed on July 6, 1919, when the
643-foot-long British Army dirigible *R34* landed
at Roosevelt Field *(photo 94).* Its crew of 30,
including 8 officers, had left East Fortune, Scot-
land, under the command of Maj. G. H. Scott, on
July 2. The 3,130-mile journey was completed in
108 hours, 12 minutes.

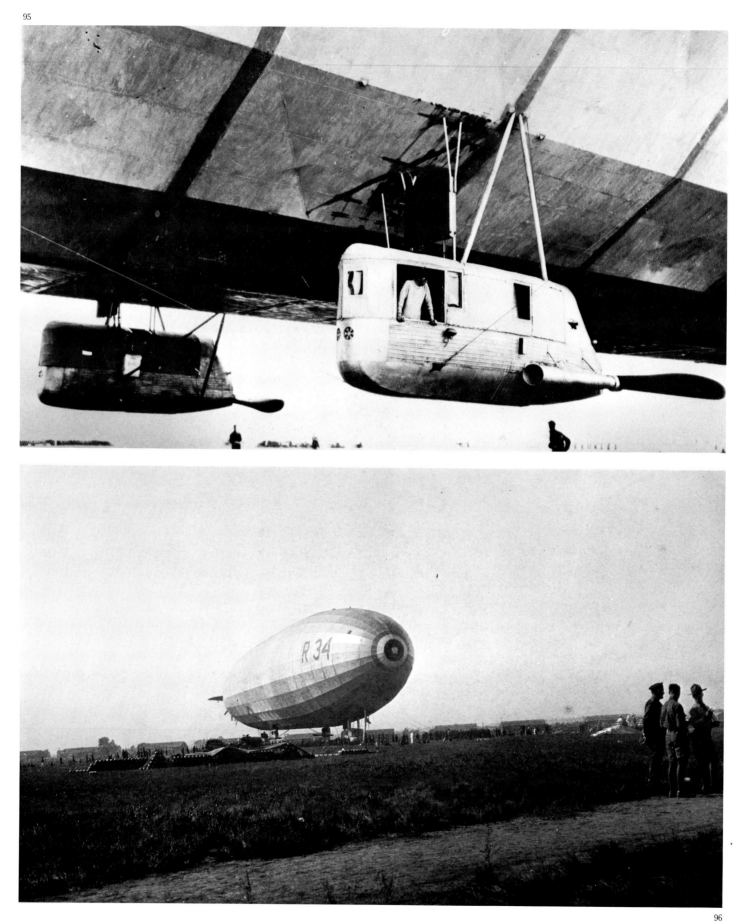

97

Besides the above-mentioned crew, the *R34* carried one more passenger: the first trans-Atlantic air stowaway, Aircraftsman William Ballantyne, seen here in the middle gondola *(photo 95)*. In order to organize a ground crew for the mooring of the *R34,* Maj. J. E. M. Pritchard, one of the officers, descended to Roosevelt Field in a parachute, thus accomplishing two firsts: he was the first person arriving in an airborne vehicle from Europe to set foot in America; and he was also the first such person to land safely by parachute from an airship. *Photographs 96 and 97* show the *R34* safely moored at Roosevelt Field. Three days later, on July 9, the mammoth airship commenced its return voyage (this time to Fulham, England) to complete the trans-Atlantic round trip. Prevailing winds made the trip back much faster: only 75 hours, 3 minutes. *(Photo 94: The Royal Aeronautical Society. Photo 95: Huntington Historical Society. Photo 96 by Henry Villard. Photo 97: John Drennan Collection.)*

98, 99. While the British and Germans were developing rigid airships during World War I, the U.S. military was building blimps—nonrigid airships—such as the U.S. Navy *C-4*, shown here at Hazelhurst Field in 1919. *(Photo 98: Huntington Historical Society. Photo 99: Glenn H. Curtiss Museum.)*

100. While the annual games of the New York Police Department were taking place at Brooklyn's Sheepshead Bay Speedway on July 28, 1919, Lt. George Burgess of the Army Air Service was flying in a Curtiss Jenny 2,000 feet overhead with Miss Emily Schaeffer of Seagate (Brooklyn). In another Jenny flying nearby was Naval Chaplain Rev. Alexander Wouters and pilot Lt. Eugene H. Barksdale. What was so unusual about this flight was that Miss Schaeffer and Lt. Burgess were being married by Rev. Wouters. It was America's first airplane wedding. Communication was by radio, at that time relatively new. In the photograph, Col. Archie Miller, commander of Hazelhurst Field, Mineola, congratulates the bride. Between them stands Miss Doris K. Schob, the maid of honor. At the left are Rev. Wouters, Lt. Barksdale (partially concealed), who was also the best man, and Lt. Burgess. *(Edward Gardyan Collection.)*

98

99

100

101–105. A major International Air Race was held from August 25 through August 27, 1919. Twenty-eight participants (11 Americans and 17 Canadians), flying various war-surplus planes, raced either from Roosevelt Field, Mineola, to the Leaside Aerodrome in Toronto, Canada, or from Toronto to Mineola, in either case stopping at Buffalo and Syracuse. The Hotel Commodore, New York, offered $10,000 in cash prizes, divided between two simultaneous contests—one for speed, the other for "reliability," with the emphasis on the latter. There were two sets of winners as a result. In addition, there was a separate list of U.S. military winners, who were not eligible for cash prizes. These multiple lists have made the event probably the least-understood race in aviation history. *101:* American aviators entered in the race consult a map at Roosevelt Field before starting, on August 25. From left to right: Lts. R. F. Midkiff, H. B. Chandler, B. H. Adams, P. Melville, W. R. Taylor, and F. A. Malony. *Photos 102 through 104* show various planes lined up at Roosevelt Field before takeoff. The plane numbered "32" in *photo 103* is a Curtiss "Jenny" entered by Dick DePew. *Photo 104* (August 26, 1919) shows the Curtiss "Oriole" (center) flown by J. D. Hill, which crashed at Albany.

105: One of the more unusual planes entered in the contest was this Italian trimotor Caproni. *(Photo 101: U.S. Air Force Museum. Photo 102: George C. Dade Collection. Photos 103 and 104: Edward Peck Collection. Photo 105: Glenn H. Curtiss Museum.)*

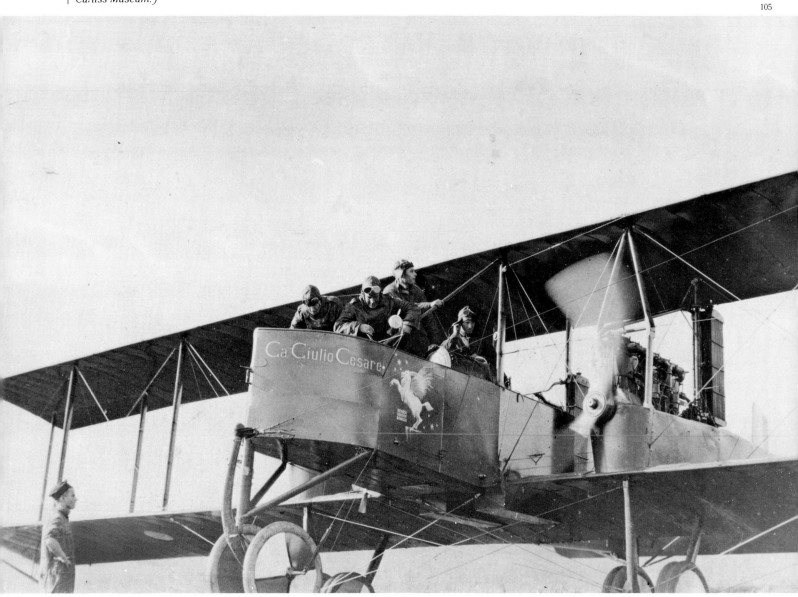

106–108. Taking off from Roosevelt Field on September 18, 1919, Roland Rohlfs, chief test pilot for the Curtiss Aeroplane and Motor Corporation, established a new world's altitude record when he climbed to 34,910 feet in a Curtiss plane of what would now seem a curious design, a Curtiss 18-T-2 "Wasp" triplane, powered by a 400-hp Kirkham K-12 engine, an extremely powerful engine for that time. In *photograph 108,* Rohlfs (right) shows the barograph to Glenn Curtiss after the flight. On the following day Rohlfs established a new rate-of-climb record, reaching 20,100 feet in ten minutes. *(Photo 106: Edward Peck Collection. Photos 107 and 108: Thomas Foxworth Collection.)*

109. After the war, development of aircraft and air services proceeded along several lines, among them the improvement of closed-cabin planes suitable for conveying passengers and the concomitant establishment of regular cross-country passenger service. This Lawson airliner is shown at Mitchel Field (a military airfield south of Roosevelt Field, opened in 1917) on September 13, 1919, after a flight from Milwaukee, Wisconsin. This was the first cross-country flight in the United States by a multi-engined passenger aircraft with a closed cabin. The airliner continued to Washington, D.C., where a number of high-ranking government officials were given rides in its 26-passenger cabin; it then returned to Milwaukee, completing a circuit of 2,500 miles. *(Glenn H. Curtiss Museum.)*

110–112. The Curtiss "Eagle" is probably the only aircraft ever made that was designed to be built with either one, two, or three engines. *Photo 110* (overleaf) shows a two-engined version under construction at the Curtiss plant on Clinton Road, Garden City, in 1919. *Photos 111 and 112* show the three-engined version, an eight-passenger airliner. On October 24, 1919, it was flown to Washington, D.C. During the ten days it was in Washington it made 82 demonstration flights and carried 476 people. Note the increasing attention to streamlining in the design of efficient airplanes evident in the "Eagle." *(Photo 110: Nassau County Museum Reference Library. Photo 111: Edward Peck Collection. Photo 112: George C. Dade Collection.)*

111

112

113, 114. This Salvation Army building *(photo 113)*, on Clinton Road in Garden City, 1918, was used during World War I to entertain the military personnel of Hazelhurst Field and Camp Mills. In 1920 it was divided in two and moved down Clinton Road to Hempstead (see photo 115). There, at the northeast corner of Washington Street and Lincoln Boulevard, the two buildings, converted to apartment houses, stand today (July 1986; see *photo 114*), the last vestige of World War I training fields on Long Island. *(Photo 113: Nassau County Museum Reference Library. Photo 114 by James C. Mooney; George C. Dade Collection.)*

115, 116. Hazelhurst Field, looking north, in 1920. Clinton Road is at the left. In the foreground, just south of Stewart Avenue, is the plant of the Curtiss Engineering Corporation. Notice the building being moved down Clinton Road, lower left. This is half of the World War I Salvation Army building shown in photo 113. The other half still had not been moved at the time of this photograph.

In 1921 Hazelhurst Field became Curtiss Field. In 1929 Curtiss Field was incorporated into Roosevelt Field (to the east of the area in *photo 115*). Flying activities ceased in 1951 to make way for the construction of Roosevelt Field Shopping Center (in 1956). This remains today, as may be seen in *photo 116* (July 1986). Macy's department store is to the right of center. The Curtiss plant has now become the Oxford plant of the Esselte Pendaflex Corporation. Few of the Roosevelt Field Shopping Center's thousands of patrons are aware as they make their purchases that they do so on the site of what not long ago was one of the most exciting aviation centers in the world. *(Photo 115: Frank Strnad Collection. Photo 116 by James C. Mooney; George C. Dade Collection.)*

114

117, 118. Where only a few years earlier a coast-to-coast flight had been an ordeal, in 1920 four army planes were able to make a round trip between New York and Alaska (including several stops) without much difficulty. On July 15, the De Havilland DH-4's left Mitchel Field, arriving in Nome, Alaska, on August 25. The return trip was begun on August 29. Two of the planes are shown here after their arrival at Mitchel Field on October 20. Actual flying time for the total distance of some 9,000 miles was 112 hours. *(Both photos: George C. Dade Collection.)*

119. In 1920 the Pulitzer brothers established a prize fund to promote aviation and encourage aircraft development in America. For six years the Pulitzer Trophy Race—open to all countries—was the number-one aviation event in the United States. The initial race was held at Mitchel Field on Thanksgiving Day, November 25, 1920. Thirty-seven participants flew and 25 finished, having been required to fly four times around a 29.02-mile triangular course. The margin of victory was claimed by Maj. Corliss C. Moseley of the U.S. Army Engineering Division, flying a Verville-Packard R-1 Racer (in the photograph) powered by a 638-hp Packard engine. Moseley's average speed was 156.5 mph. *(National Air and Space Museum.)*

120. At 4:50 P.M., February 23, 1921, Ernest Allison landed his DH-4 at Hazelhurst Field, completing the first transcontinental-airmail test flights. Allison was the last in a chain of six pilots to convey a load of mail from San Francisco to New York. Flying continuously, day and night, the winged pony express took 33 hours, 21 minutes to deliver the mail—almost three full days faster than the best time by rail. *(National Air and Space Museum.)*

121. The Curtiss "Eagle" shown here in its one-engined version, used as a U.S. Army ambulance plane (March 5, 1921). *(Nassau County Museum Reference Library).*

Maj. Christie greeting Lt. E. C. Nutt the second to land. Alaska Flying Exp.

Oct. 20, 1920.

122

122. Hazelhurst Field, occupying the western portion of what was formerly the Hempstead Plains Aerodrome, was purchased by the Curtiss Corporation in 1920. On May 15, 1921 (see photograph), the field was reopened under the new name of Curtiss Field. It continued under this name through 1929, when it was incorporated into Roosevelt Field. *(Nassau County Museum Reference Library.)*

123, 124. Streamlining, increased power, and practical serviceability for passenger transport all received attention in the 1920s. In 1921, the Remington-Burnelli Company of Amityville built a 20-passenger airliner that boasted a cabin 14 feet wide and 20 feet long, the largest to date in any airplane. The fuselage, shaped as an airfoil, offered less resistance to the air, and two 400-hp Liberty engines provided ample power. The biplane, with a 70-foot wingspan, is seen here at Curtiss Field *(photo 123)* and flying over Long Island *(photo 124)* in the summer of 1921. *(Photo 123: National Air and Space Museum. Photo 124: Nassau County Museum Reference Library.)*

123

124

125. Bert Acosta (1895–1954), who soon came much into the public eye for his daredevil antics and romantic swagger (a swagger, some said, induced more by spirits than by spirit), captured the 1921 Pulitzer Trophy for the Curtiss Corporation by flying the Curtiss R-1 (seen here at Curtiss Field in 1921, some time after the October 1 race) at a speed of 176.6 mph. Acosta proved the superiority of the small streamlined racer over the more powerful but less well aerodynamically adapted aircraft favored by some. *(George C. Dade Collection.)*

126. On December 29, 1921, Edward Stinson, of the famous family of fliers, and Lloyd Bertaud, another well-known pilot, took off from Roosevelt Field in an open-cockpit, all-metal Junkers-Larsen JL-6 monoplane and circled Long Island in a snowstorm and below-freezing temperatures. When the aircraft landed where it had departed from (see photo), at 11:17 A.M., after 26 hours, 19 minutes, 7 seconds of continuous flying, Stinson and Bertaud had broken the world endurance record by two hours. *(John Drennan Collection.)*

127–129. Lawrence Sperry, responsible for many "firsts" in the history of flight, was probably also the first air commuter. He called his civilian M-1 "Messenger" (designed by Alfred Verville) his "air flivver" and used it to commute from his home in Garden City to the Lawrence Sperry Company plant in Farmingdale (he had left his father's company to branch out on his own in 1917). *127:* The "air flivver" in Sperry's garage at Garden City, winter 1921. *128:* The air flivver next to Sperry's automobile, Garden City, summer 1922. (Sperry once said that though the initial cost of his airplane and car was about the same, the plane, "mile for mile, is pleasanter, easier, and cheaper to operate.") *129:* The original military version of the Sperry M-1 "Messenger" with Sperry and guests (exact date and place of photograph unknown). This small biplane had only a 20-foot wingspan; it was powered with a 64-hp engine. Designed by Verville for carrying dispatches, it was called by Gen. William ("Billy") Mitchell, Chief of the Army Air Service, "the motorcycle of the air." *(Photos 127 and 128: National Air and Space Museum. Photo 129: Thomas Foxworth Collection.)*

133

134

The dramatic contrast is seen in *photo 133,* where its 106-foot wingspan overshadows the 20-foot wingspan of a Sperry "Messenger," the smallest army aircraft. With three engines that developed a total of 1,200 hp, this monster of an airplane was designed as a bomber, and it was dubbed the "Owl" because it was also intended for night flying. *Photo 134* shows it in flight over Curtiss Field (late 1922; *photo 135* at Mitchel Field, same period). Despite its power, the "Owl" failed to live up to its promise, showing poor flight characteristics; it was officially scrapped in 1923. *(Photo 132: Nassau County Museum Reference Library. Photo 133: Thomas Foxworth Collection. Photo 134: National Air and Space Museum. Photo 135: Frank Strnad Collection.)*

136, 137. Air technology had so improved since Cal Rodgers' madcap transcontinental flight of 1911 that it was natural to expect that sooner or later somebody would attempt the coast-to-coast flight nonstop. On May 2, 1923 (after two previous attempts, beginning from the West Coast, had failed), two Army Air Service pilots left Roosevelt Field and, 26 hours and 50 minutes later, made a successful landing at Rockwell Field, San Diego, California. They were greeted by base commander Maj. Henry J. ("Hap") Arnold, later chief of the U.S. Army Air Force in World War II. The fliers, Lts. John A. Macready and Oakley G. Kelly, are seen here *(photo 137),* undaunted by their previous failures, with their Army Fokker T-2 monoplane at Roosevelt Field before takeoff. *(Photo 136: Frank Strnad Collection. Photo 137: U.S. Air Force Museum.)*

135

143

142. The Air Meet at Mitchel Field, July 4, 1924, with an extraordinary attendance of 75,000, was remarkable in many ways, reflecting the many sides of aviation at the time. The appearance of Lt. Russell Maughan brought to mind his recent dawn-to-dusk flight across the continent. There were demonstrations of trick flying, races, parachute jumping, bombing of temporary structures, a demonstration of skywriting, and other displays by military and civilian fliers. Capt. Charles Nungesser (1892–1927), the renowned French ace, put in an appearance, conjuring up visions of the recent heroism of the flying aces of World War I. (When Capt. Nungesser was lost in an attempted east-west Atlantic crossing in 1927, all France mourned.) *(Frank Strnad Collection.)*

143. Capt. Nungesser, smiling for the camera, stands before the propeller of his Potez light plane, one of a number of aircraft he brought to the U.S. for show work. Mitchel Field, June 1924, before the Air Meet. *(Nassau County Museum Reference Library.)*

144–147. Development of fighter planes and racers was paralleled by that of commercial aircraft along eminently practical lines, with day-to-day use in mind. In August 1924 the Remington-Burnelli Aircraft Corporation built at their Maspeth, Queens, factory an improved version of their 1921 RB-1 passenger airliner. The twin-engined RB-2 freight airplane was built entirely of the alloy duralumin, including the covering of the 80-foot wings. Powered by two 500-hp Galloway "Atlantic" engines, the plane could exceed 100 mph carrying its full payload of three tons. Great publicity attended the debut of this first practical cargo plane at Curtiss Field, early August 1924 *(photos 144, 145).*

148

146: The RB-2 flying over long Island. *147:* A 1924 Essex Coupe inside the fuselage of the RB-2. It was said that the car's engine had been removed. Note the golf clubs next to the spare tire. *(Photo 146: Frank Strnad Collection. Other photos: National Air and Space Museum.)*

148, 149. Scarcely five years after the conquest of the Atlantic by air, a successful circuit of the entire globe was made by two U.S. Army planes (out of four that started) under the command of Col. Lowell H. Smith, with the entire operation directed by Maj. Gen. Mason Patrick. Four Douglas World Cruisers, the *Seattle*, the *Chicago*, the *Boston,* and the *New Orleans,* each carrying two men, departed from Seattle, Washington, on April 6, 1924. (Crew members were Frederick Martin, Alva Harvey [*Seattle*], Lowell Smith, Leslie Arnold [*Chicago*], Leigh Wade, Henry Ogden [*Boston*], Eric Nelson, and John Harding [*New Orleans*].) After flying a zigzag course of over 26,000 miles, the *Chicago* and the *New Orleans* returned to their starting point on September 28; accompanying them was a new plane, the *Boston II,* a replacement for the *Boston* (which had been wrecked near Iceland) manned by its crew. The *Seattle* had cracked up in Alaska (luckily its crew was rescued) early in the venture. New York was one of many stops made by the three other planes. On September 8, they touched down at Mitchel Field (the *Chicago* is seen landing in *photo 148*), where the visiting Prince of Wales and a large crowd gave them a rousing welcome. *Photo 149* (over-leaf) shows the three planes flying low over New York City on the same day. *(Photo 148 by Joseph Burt; John Drennan Collection. Photo 149: U.S. Air Force Museum and George C. Dade Collection.)*

150–152. Airplanes continued to gain in their ability to cut through the air with streamlined ease. On September 27, 1924, this Navy Curtiss R2C-2 racer was flown by Lt. David Rittenhouse *(photo 151)* at Port Washington, on the north shore of Nassau County. The Navy pilot there attained a speed of 227.5 mph, an unofficial seaplane speed record. He was preparing to enter his racer in the upcoming Schneider Cup contest but the race was canceled when foreign competition withdrew. *152:* The R2C-2 being prepared for flight. *(Photo 150: Nassau County Museum Reference Library. Photos 151 and 152: William Wait, Jr. Collection.)*

150

153-156. In April 1925 Capt. Charles Nungesser
starred as himself in the film *The Sky Raider,* a
melodrama filled with crime, love, justice, and
above all aviation acrobatics, disaster, and
heroism. This seven-reel feature film, one of a
growing number of movies about the world of
airplanes and their pilot heroes, was filmed by
Encore Pictures at Roosevelt Field in the fall
and winter of 1924–25. *153:* Director T. Hayes
Hunter explains a camera angle to Nungesser
and skywriting pilot Lou Meier. Note the German
Cross insignia (half blocked by Hunter) on the
Curtiss Jenny camera plane. *154:* Capt. Nungesser's plane used in *The Sky Raider,* a French
Hanriot HD-1 World War I fighter. Roosevelt
Field. *155:* The cast and crew of *The Sky Raider*
on location. Among those in the photo are Carl
"Slim" Hennicke, wing walker and mechanic
(standing, third from left), Lou Meier (fourth
from left), T. Hayes Hunter (sixth from left),
Charles Nungesser (eighth from left), and, of
particular interest in retrospect, the famous
Russian aircraft designer and helicopter pioneer, Igor Sikorsky (standing, far right).

156: Lou Meier sprays message-writing smoke from his Skywriting Corporation of America plane (a British S.E. 5a), Roosevelt Field, late 1924. Skywriting was invented by Maj. Jack C. Savage of the British Royal Air Force and first demonstrated on May 30, 1922. Soon the American Allan J. Cameron made an arrangement with Maj. Savage to bring skywriting to the United States, and the Skywriting Corporation of America was formed. Skywriting is a very difficult art. Letters must be formed with great care and precision at an altitude of ten or twelve thousand feet. The smoke used is created by controlled mixing of a special oil with the plane's exhaust. Used chiefly for advertising, the art has survived to the present day, although what most people see in the sky today is actually a modernized, electronically controlled version of skywriting known as "skytyping," using a flight of five aircraft. *(Photo 156 by*

Court Commercial Photo. All photos: Nassau County Museum Reference Library.)
157–160. The Curtiss Corporation also built many a military plane on wheels rather than pontoons, suitable for use on land. At times Curtiss seemed to monopolize the field: at the last of the Pulitzer Trophy races, held at Mitchel Field on October 12, 1925, both Army and Navy competitors flew these specially built Curtiss R3C-1 racers. The winner was Army Lt. Cyrus ("Cy") Bettis, speed 248.9 mph; Navy Lt. Alford J. ("Al") Williams (1896–1958), speed 241 mph, came in second place. *157:* Lt. Bettis' plane (no. 43). *158:* Lt. Williams' plane (no. 40). *159:* Judges wave to Lt. Bettis as he passes the home pylon. *160:* Lt. Bettis (left) and Lt. Williams. *(Photos 157 and 158 by Frank La Vista; Carl "Slim" Hennicke Collection. Photos 159 and 160: Thomas Foxworth Collection.)*

164–166. After the First World War, the "barn-stormers" flourished, spreading the thrill of flight by traveling around the country giving flight demonstrations, performing daredevil stunts in the air, and taking people for rides. *164:* Barnstormers getting ready to do a "wing walking" stunt on a Curtiss "Jenny" at a Curtiss Field air show, 1926. The Jenny, built as a war training and reconnaissance plane, was the most popular plane of the barnstormers. Plenty of surplus Jennies were available at low cost after the war, they were safe and maneuverable, and they were easily serviced. *165:* A Standard SJ-1 (foreground, Roosevelt Field, 1926), another favorite of the barnstormers. A Curtiss Jenny may be seen behind it. *166:* Intrepid air-men enjoying a hot dog while waiting for customers at Roosevelt Field, 1926. Note the offer: "Fly $5.00." After World War I, many trained aviators had no outlet for their flying skills other than barnstorming. *(Photo 164: Frank Strnad Collection. Photos 165 and 166: Carl "Slim" Hennicke Collection.)*

168

169

167–174. In the 1920s, increasingly daring feats of aviation were attempted—often ending in disaster. A major incentive to such frenetic flying activity was the famous Orteig prize. In 1919, Raymond Orteig, a Frenchman who owned two hotels in New York, offered $25,000 to the first person to fly nonstop between New York and Paris. One of the more dramatic—and tragic—failures to capture the Orteig prize was that of Captain René Fonck, the most famous of French war aces, who, with a crew of three, took off from Roosevelt Field on September 21, 1926, amid much fanfare. His specially designed Sikorsky S-35 biplane, carrying 2,300 gallons of fuel, crashed over a twenty-foot drop separating Roosevelt Field from Curtiss Field, and the plane was engulfed in flames. Jacob Isliamoff, the mechanic, and Charles Clavier, the radio operator, failed to escape from their posts in the fuselage and were killed. Lt. Lawrence M. Curtin, the copilot and navigator, and Fonck himself managed to escape. The primary cause of the crash was believed to have been the premature release of the left set of auxiliary wheels, which damaged the left rudder. *167:* Fonck's plane on a test flight. *168:* At 2 P.M. on September 8, 1926, New York's Mayor James J. ("Jimmy") Walker christened Fonck's plane in front of a huge crowd of aviation enthusiasts. *169:* The official party lined up after the christening ceremony (from left to right): Bernard Sandler, Rev. Richard O. Pope (pastor of the Protestant Episcopal Church of Westbury), Lt. Allan Snody, Mayor Walker, Capt. Fonck, and Igor Sikorsky, builder of the plane.

171

173

174

170: Fonck's Sikorsky S-35 on Roosevelt Field. *171:* A left rear view of the plane, showing the auxiliary landing gear that failed to remain in position and caused the crash. *172:* Fonck's plane before takeoff, Roosevelt Field, September 21, 1926. *173:* Front view of the Sikorsky before takeoff, showing the barrels that contained the plane's 2,300 gallons of fuel. *174:* The charred remains of Fonck's plane after the disaster. *(Photo 167 courtesy of The Queens Borough Public Library. Photo 168 by Court Commercial Photo; Paul Rizzo Collection. Photo 169: National Air and Space Museum. Photos 170, 172, and 174: Frank Strnad Collection. Photo 171: Paul Rizzo Collection. Photo 173: George C. Dade Collection.)*

176

175. Crowds of automobiles on the sidelines at the American Legion Air Circus, Curtiss Field, Sunday afternoon, September 26, 1926. The large airplane on the right is the Remington-Burnelli RB-2. *(Frank Strnad Collection.)*

176–180. One of the major designers and manufacturers of aircraft designed for practical civilian purposes was the Fairchild Airplane Manufacturing Corporation, which opened its factory in the former Sperry facilities in Farmingdale, on the Nassau-Suffolk County border, in 1926. For over twenty years, Fairchild Utility Monoplanes were used for everything from carrying mail to exploring the South Pole. The prototype, the FC-1, was introduced on June 14, 1926. Refitted with a much more powerful engine (a 200-hp Wright J-4), the FC-1 was reintroduced on January 8, 1927, as the FC-1A. *176:* Publicity photo for the introduction of the FC-1A, Curtiss Field, January 1927. The monoplane had a 44-foot wingspan; its wings could be folded. *177:* Interior of the Fairchild factory, with the FC-2 under construction, summer of 1927. Note the woman worker sewing the fabric on the control surface. Whereas the FC-1/1A was the prototype, only one plane having been made, a number of the similar FC-2/2C planes were made for use in the U.S. and Canada. *178:* Aerial view of the Fairchild factory on Fulton Street, Farmingdale, October 29, 1927.

183: After the successful flight, Roosevelt Field, April 14, 1927. *(Photo 181: Nassau County Museum Reference Library. Photo 182: Frank Strnad Collection. Photo 183 by Joseph Burt; John Drennan Collection.)*

183

184, 185. Among those fliers known to have had their eyes set on Europe were Clarence D. Chamberlin; Comdr. Richard E. Byrd, famous for his daring flight over the North Pole the previous year; and an until-recently obscure airmail pilot named Charles A. Lindbergh, who had suddenly leaped into public recognition by flying across the United States in record time. *184:* Chamberlin and Lindbergh on the porch of the Garden City Hotel, comparing various routes from New York to Paris (May 1927). *185:* Lindbergh, Byrd, and Chamberlin in a hangar at Curtiss Field, in front of Lindbergh's plane the *Spirit of St. Louis* (May 1927). *(Photo 184: Garden City Archives. Photo 185: George C. Dade Collection.)*

186. Lindbergh standing in front of the *Spirit of St. Louis*, Curtiss Field, May 1927. Lindbergh's aircraft was a custom-designed Ryan NYP monoplane. Claude Ryan of San Diego had become known as a designer of planes that were safe and reliable on overnight mail runs. Lindbergh joined Ryan and his aeronautical engineer Donald A. Hall in San Diego in February 1927 and personally supervised the construction of the *Spirit of St. Louis,* including a Wright "Whirlwind" engine and added fuel tanks for the projected flight of over three thousand miles. *(Garden City Archives.)*

184

185

186

187

187. The Bellanca WB-2, now named *Columbia* (often later also called the *Miss Columbia*), at Curtiss Field, May 20, 1927, the day of Lindbergh's flight. The words "New York to Paris" on the fuselage openly proclaimed the intention to attempt the crossing. The flight was delayed, however, while the plane's owner, Charles A. Levine, wrangled with a number of prospective pilots about the route and other details. (*Frank Strnad Collection.*)

188. While the fate of the *Columbia* remained uncertain, Charles Lindbergh, working alone, quietly proceeded with his own plans. This photograph, taken at Curtiss Field a few days before the takeoff for Paris, shows the *Spirit of St. Louis* surrounded by an admiring and expectant crowd. (*Frank Strnad Collection.*)

189. Portrait of Charles A. Lindbergh, Jr. Lindbergh began his career no differently from dozens of other young aviators, with a few essential differences: he was known for his sobriety—in more than one sense—and was thoroughly conversant with the requirements of flying and with the capabilities and flightworthiness of various airplanes. Born in Detroit on February 4, 1902, the son of a U.S. Congressman, Lindbergh attended the University of Wisconsin. He learned to fly in 1922, purchased his own Curtiss Jenny and became a barnstormer for a while, and then a flying cadet in the U.S. Air Reserve in 1925. In 1926 he worked as an air-mail pilot on the route between Chicago and St. Louis.

After his famous solo trans-Atlantic flight, personal tragedy—the kidnapping and murder of his two-year-old son—placed Lindbergh in the public eye once again. Both before and after this calamity, he made many further contributions to flying and its application to other fields. Among a great number of accomplishments, he invented valuable flying aids, contributed to the design of important planes, and helped obtain funding for the rocket experiments of Robert H. Goddard in 1929. With his wife, Anne Morrow Lindbergh, he also made many significant aerial surveys and pioneering flights in many parts of the world. A prize-winning author of many books, and decorated many times over for his contributions to aviation, Lindbergh died in Hawaii on August 26, 1974. (*Minnesota Historical Society.*)

[104]

189

188

190

191

192

190. The *Spirit of St. Louis* being wheeled across Curtiss Field. On May 20, 1927, the plane was towed up a ramp to Roosevelt Field, where it took off into an east wind, in a light rain, at 7:52 A.M. The rest is history: 33 hours, 30 minutes later, Lindbergh made a perfect landing at Le Bourget Field, near Paris, at 10:22 P.M., Paris time, having covered the 3,610 miles at an average speed of 108 mph. This New York-Paris hop not only earned Lindbergh the $25,000 Orteig prize but also made him, almost literally overnight, an international celebrity. Though "Lucky Lindy" had been favored by good flying weather (and had undoubtedly been in the right place at the right time), any flight of such a distance, especially over water, in those days, was an exceedingly risky venture, particularly for one man, leading the press to bestow on Lindbergh the additional epithet of "Flyin' Fool" following his solo takeoff.

But luck was only partly responsible for Lindbergh's success, nor was he the fool some journalists made him out to be. His skill as a navigator was such that, flying through sleet, fog, and darkness, and without a radio—purely by dead reckoning—by the time he had reached the southwest coast of Ireland he was still within three miles of his originally charted course. Devoting close attention to every detail, Lindbergh planned and executed his venture as expertly as any pioneer before him.

In any case, Charles Lindbergh succeeded where others had failed. His success was given sensational treatment by the press (headlines were the equivalent of those used to announce the declaration of a world war!), and, like no other aviator before or since, the "Lone Eagle" was hailed as a hero and heaped with honors on both sides of the ocean he had been the first to fly alone. *(Nassau County Museum Reference Library.)*

191. Unwilling to be "scooped" and lose the film footage of the decade, this Fox News photographer armed with a movie camera recorded Lindbergh's departure from an aerial vantage point on the morning of May 20. Fog and rain prevented the photographer from getting clear shots, but at least pilot George Wies could be the last to dip the wing of his plane, a Curtiss "Oriole," in an aviator's salute to the Paris-bound Lindy. *(George C. Dade Collection.)*

192. The Bellanca *Columbia* ready for takeoff at Roosevelt Field, June 4, 1927. Charles Levine had by this time ironed out his problems. Apparently chagrined by Lindbergh's success, he decided to make a mystery of the *Columbia*'s precise destination (note that the words "to Paris" on the fuselage have been painted over). Clarence Chamberlin, an experienced and reliable flier, was finally chosen as the pilot. At the last minute, Levine—a millionaire businessman and aviation enthusiast—created a sensation by accompanying Chamberlin to become the world's first trans-Atlantic airplane passenger (for a short distance, having had some prior flying experience himself, he relieved Chamberlin at the controls). This crossing did not go as smoothly as Lindbergh's. The compass broke when they were near Cape Cod. What followed is one of the curiosities of aviation history: the ingenious Chamberlin followed the ocean liner *Mauretania* and then calculated their position based on a knowledge of the liner's departure time! *(Frank Strnad Collection.)*

193. Forty-two hours and 45 minutes after take-off, on June 6, Chamberlin and Levine made a forced landing in a wheat field near Eisleben, Germany. Their original secret goal had been Berlin, but still they had traveled 3,911 miles, a new world record. Eventually they made it to Berlin, where they received a rousing welcome. *(Frank Strnad Collection.)*

194. On June 16, 1927, twelve days after Chamberlin and Levine's departure from Roosevelt Field, Lindbergh returned triumphantly, as this sea of humanity shows. *(Photo by Joseph Burt; John Drennan Collection.)*

195. An aerial view of the thousands of automobiles arranged in a circle at Roosevelt Field on the day of Lindbergh's return from Europe. *(Frank Strnad Collection.)*

195A. The same site today (July 1986). At left of center is the oval track of Roosevelt Raceway. Some of the stores of the Roosevelt Field Shopping Center may be seen at the extreme left. *(Photo by James C. Mooney; George C. Dade Collection.)*

195

196

197

198

199

196-199. Comdr. (later Rear Adm.) Richard E. Byrd, the famous explorer, was the third major competitor for trans-Atlantic honors in 1927 (but not for the Orteig prize, in which he showed no interest and for which he had not entered). Known for his thoroughness, Byrd carefully planned every detail of the flight. Bert Acosta was chosen as pilot and there was also a relief pilot, Bernt Balchen, and a flight engineer, Lt. George O. Noville. Their plane was a Fokker Tri-Motor with three Wright engines, named the *America.*

Byrd and his crew took off from Roosevelt Field at 5:24 A.M., June 29, 1927, New York time, bound for Le Bourget Field, Paris. Theirs was a much more difficult flight than even Chamberlin's and Levine's. Long before they made it to the French coast, they hit a bank of impenetrable fog. They managed to make it to a point over Paris and were heard by radio at Le Bourget Field, but night had fallen and since those were still the days before adequate night flying was possible, they were unable to land. With the fuel running out, their situation was becoming more dangerous by the minute. Here it was Byrd's foresight and ingenuity that saved their lives: they flew all the way back to the Atlantic Ocean, made an emergency landing in the water off Ver-sur-Mer, and paddled to shore in a rubber life raft. They spent the night as guests of

the city of Caen and were then taken to Paris. *196:* The *America* in front of its hangar at Roosevelt Field before the flight. *197:* Another view of the *America.* The man in white knickers is Bert Acosta. *198:* The *America* just before take-off from a specially built ramp at the east end of Roosevelt Field. Byrd had offered the use of this ramp to Lindbergh, but the wind was blowing in the wrong direction on the day of Lindbergh's flight. *199:* The *America* at takeoff. *(Photo 196: William Wildhagen Collection. Photo 197: Frank Strnad Collection. Photo 198 by Joseph Burt; John Drennan Collection. Photo 199: Nassau County Museum Reference Library.)*

213

214

215

213–215. Aviation history is filled with bizarre tragedies. The story of the *Bonney Gull* is one of them. This curious monoplane, designed by Leonard W. Bonney (1886–1928), a Wright-trained pilot, incorporated several features of the flight of gulls. By hydraulically altering the position and angle of the wings in flight, and expanding the elevators, the plane could be made to take off and land in an extremely confined space. On its first flight, May 4, 1928, at Curtiss Field (*photos 213* and *214* show the plane at Mitchel Field), Bonney did manage to take off in a very short distance—300 feet—and climb quickly to an altitude of 80 feet. But the *Bonney Gull* then suddenly nosed down and plummeted into a nearby golfcourse *(photo 215)*, killing the pilot and his hopes to emulate the flight of birds. *(Photo 213: National Air and Space Museum. Photo 214: Jim Boss Collection. Photo 215: A. J. "Jack" McRae Collection.)*
216. Proud and determined members of the Brooklyn Aero Club pose with their new Waco 10 at Curtiss Field, June 30, 1928. *(Photo by Joseph Burt; courtesy of The Queens Borough Public Library.)*

216

217. John Henry Mears and Capt. Charles B. D. Collyer at Curtiss Field, July 22, 1928, having just traveled around the world in 23 days, 15 hours, 21 minutes (partly, but not entirely by air), thus effectively "racing the moon" around the globe. Their plane, the *City of New York*, was a Fairchild FC-2W cabin monoplane powered by a 400-hp Pratt & Whitney "Wasp" engine. Mears—like so many fliers from the beginning to the present, an amateur—was a theatrical manager and producer whose avocation was circumnavigating the world in record time (he held several records); Collyer was an airmail pilot, skywriter, and test pilot. *(William Kaiser Collection.)*
218, 219. Many now-famous aircraft manufacturers began their operations in the late 1920s and 1930s. The structurally and aerodynamically advanced Lockheed "Vega," the first of Lock-

heed's many great airplanes, was used by a number of renowned fliers in their record-setting activities. On August 19–20, 1928, a Vega named the *Yankee Doodle* was flown by pilot Art Goebel and Santa Monica businessman Harry J. Tucker nonstop from Los Angeles to New York in the record time of 18 hours, 58 minutes. *218:* The *Yankee Doodle* after landing at Curtiss Field. *219:* Tucker and Goebel. *(Photo 218 courtesy of The Queens Borough Public Library. Photo 219: George C. Dade Collection and Nassau County Museum Reference Library.)*
220. Comdr. Richard E. Byrd's Fairchild FC-2W2, the *Stars and Stripes*, at Mitchel Field, summer 1928. Byrd took this plane to Antarctica, where he logged 146 hours of photo-mapping flights in it, beginning January 15, 1929. The plane was left in the Antarctic ice, dug out four years later,

and used for 41 more hours of photo mapping—a credit to the remarkable durability of Fairchild Utility Monoplanes. The *Stars and Stripes* has survived the years, and, rebuilt by volunteers, is now on display at the Cradle of Aviation Museum at Mitchel Field. *(Photo by Joseph Burt; courtesy of The Queens Public Library.)*
221. The Bellanca *Roma* (with a 525-hp Pratt & Whitney engine) at Roosevelt Field, September 14, 1928, before taking off for Old Orchard Beach, Maine, on the first leg of a flight to Rome. The *Roma*, flown by the American Roger Q. Williams and the Italian Cesare Sabelli, made it to Maine, and even took off for Europe, but soon returned when, for various reasons, they decided to abandon the flight. *(Photo by Joseph Burt; courtesy of The Queens Borough Public Library.)*

219

220

221

222

223

222. In the late summer of 1928, Fairchild opened a new factory and airfield in East Farmingdale, shown in this photograph (in the fall, slightly after the opening). The main building still stands, having been used almost continuously for the manufacture of aircraft through December 1987, when Fairchild, now Fairchild Republic (a division of Fairchild Industries), ceased manufacturing aircraft in East Farmingdale. *(Frank Strnad Collection and Republic Aviation Corporation.)*

223. The official opening of the new Fairchild Aircraft Corporation plant, East Farmingdale, late summer, 1928. The adjoining airfield still exists as Republic Airport. *(Jim Boss Collection and Fairchild Industries.)*

224. The new Fairchild 71s produced at the new East Farmingdale plant. Note the folding wings for ease in hangar storage. *(Jim Boss Collection and Fairchild Industries.)*

225. Fairchild-manufactured floats being attached to a Fairchild FC-2W-1 at Hulse Brothers Boat Yard, Amityville, October 1928. Fairchild aircraft were very popular in Canada. This one was sold to Canadian Transcontinental Airways Ltd. of Quebec City. *(Nassau County Museum Reference Library).*

224

226, 227. Elinor Smith (1911–) was a marvel among aviators, male or female. In May 1927 she soloed at Roosevelt Field—when she was fifteen years old! The following year she received an international pilot's license, becoming the youngest licensed pilot in the world. She also set a number of other records for women's firsts, as well as the women's solo endurance record, which stands to this day. She is the only pilot ever to have flown under all four of New York City's East River bridges. She worked as a test pilot for Fairchild and Bellanca. In October 1930 she was voted the Best Woman Pilot in the United States. Not long afterwards she retired from flying for a number of years to raise a family. In 1981, she related her remarkable experiences in an autobiography, *Aviatrix. 226:* Elinor Smith at Curtiss Field, 1928, the world's youngest licensed pilot at age sixteen. *227:* Flying over Long Island to set the women's solo endurance record. On April 24–25, 1929, she remained aloft in her Bellanca "Pacemaker" monoplane for 26 hours, 21 minutes, 32 seconds. Inset at right: Before takeoff. She brought with her 209½ gallons of gas and a supply of apples and oranges. Inset at left: A closeup of a jubilant Elinor Smith just after landing. *(Both photos: National Air and Space Museum.)*

228. In an attempt to break the world's refueling endurance flight record, Martin Jensen and two others took off from Roosevelt Field on the night of May 22, 1929, in the Bellanca monoplane the *Three Musketeers.* A fuel leak and damaged fuselage forced a landing before breaking the record, but not before New York *Daily News* aerial photographer Herbert McCorey could take this remarkable photograph of Jensen attempting to repair the fuel leak—clinging to the engine in the full blast of the propeller's backwash, hundreds of feet in the air. *(National Air and Space Museum.)*

229. French aviators Armand Lotti, Jean Assolant, and René Lefèvre with their Bernard 191 monoplane the *Yellow Bird* at Roosevelt Field, mid-June 1929, while the compass of their plane was being "swung" (calibrated). The three flew to Old Orchard, Maine, and then set out for Paris on June 13. After 29 hours, 52 minutes, and 3,128 miles, a fuel shortage forced the team down at Comillas, Spain. Along the way they also made a discovery: a stowaway named Arthur Schreiber! *(Photo by Court Commercial Photo; Frank Strnad Collection.)*

230. This unusual photograph of tragedy marks the end of another noble attempt to beat an endurance record. At 6:13 A.M., June 28, 1929, Viola Gentry (1900–1988) and Jack Ashcraft's Paramount "Cabinaire" biplane *The Answer* (named as a challenge to the Army's record-setting plane *The Question Mark*) crashed in the Hicks Nursery on Jericho Turnpike in Old Westbury. They had planned to surpass a record of 150 hours, 40 minutes, but ran out of gas in less than 10 hours. Ground fog had prevented the takeoff of the plane that was to have refueled theirs. Ashcraft was killed; Gentry was seriously injured but survived. *(Photo by Joseph Burt; courtesy of The Queens Borough Public Library.)*

231–233. On June 27, 1929, Capt. Frank Hawks

(1897–1938), fast becoming one of the most famous test pilots in the world, flew nonstop from Roosevelt Field to Los Angeles in record time, 19 hours, 10 minutes. He immediately turned around and made the flight the other way, this time in 17 hours, 38 minutes, another record. As a one-stop round trip, the flight time was also a record, totaling 36 hours, 48 minutes of flying time and 42 hours, 48 minutes of total elapsed time. Adding to the accomplishment was the fact that weather conditions had been very bad. Hawks flew for Texaco (The Texas Company) in a Lockheed "Air Express" powered by a 425-hp "Wasp" engine with new duralumin cowling for streamlining, a plane of the most advanced design with a full array of

gauges and instruments and a radio. On landing at Roosevelt Field on the night of June 29, Hawks plowed into a fence. He was unhurt, however, and his plane, named simply the *Texaco No. 5*, only slightly damaged. These photographs of Hawks and his plane at Roosevelt Field were evidently taken somewhat later, probably on June 30. Note the lettering proclaiming the plane the "transcontinental non-stop record holder." Upon landing and leaving the plane he had immediately fallen asleep on his wife's shoulder, but he seems to have recovered nicely for the camera. *(Photo 231 by John Drennan; George C. Dade Collection. Photo 232: Texaco, Inc. Photo 233: Carl "Slim" Hennicke Collection.)*

231

233

232

234. Miss Uva Kinney (left) and Billy Bomar (right) on the wings of a Waco 10 piloted by Paul Rizzo over Barren Island Airport, July 7, 1929. (Barren Island Airport, along the far end of Flatbush Avenue, Brooklyn, later became Floyd Bennett Field, a municipal airport, and is now part of Gateway National Recreation Area.) Rizzo, operator of Barren Island Airport, would stage air shows including stunts like this to attract customers to the airfield. Billy Bomar died in a parachute jump, when his chute failed to open, a few years after this photo was taken. Uva Kinney married and moved to New Jersey. Paul Rizzo is still an active pilot today (1989). *(Frank Strnad Collection.)*

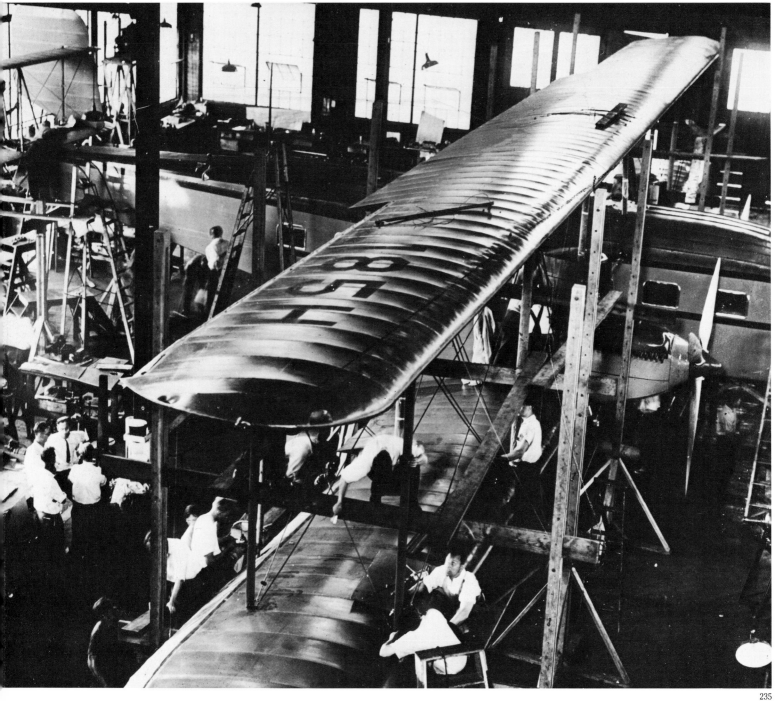

235-237. Three views of the Curtiss "Condor," the latest attempt (in 1929) to achieve new levels of luxury and comfort in commercial passenger transport. Powered by two 635-hp liquid-cooled Curtiss "Conqueror" engines, this commercial version of the Army's B-2 bomber could carry 18 passengers at a cruising speed of 120 mph. It enabled Transcontinental Air Transport (or TAT, a predecessor of TWA) to offer fast Eastern schedules. *235:* The Condor under construction in the spring of 1929 at the Garden City plant of the Curtiss Aeroplane and Motor Corporation. *236:* A front view of the Condor, revealing its impressive wingspan of 91 feet 8 inches (it was 57 feet 1 inch long). *237:* The Condor in flight near Roosevelt Field on or about July 21, 1929, its first day in the air. It is decorated with Transcontinental Air Transport markings. *(Photo 235: Nassau County Museum Reference Library. Photo 236: William Wildhagen Collection. Photo 237 by Court Commercial Photo; George C. Dade Collection.)*

237

238

238. This charming photograph of Fay Gillis and her Curtiss "Fledgling" was taken at Curtiss Field, Valley Stream, in August 1929. This Curtiss Field is not to be confused with the Garden City airport of the same name, which was incorporated into Roosevelt Field in this year. The Valley Stream airport was opened on April 7, 1929, in southwestern Nassau County, just across the New York City line. It had a very brief history: in 1930, it was the busiest commercial airfield on Long Island, but various factors, including the depression, forced its closing in 1933, and eventually Green Acres Shopping Center was built on the site. It was at this Curtiss Field that Costes and Bellonte completed the first nonstop Paris-to-New York trans-Atlantic flight, in 1930.

In September, Fay Gillis had a flying accident when the tail assembly of her Fledgling collapsed during a demonstration. She bailed out by parachute, qualifying her for the Caterpillar Club, an organization sponsored by the Irvin Air Chute Company to honor pilots who had saved their lives by parachute. She was the second woman member. Miss Gillis then became an airplane saleswoman, possibly the very first, working for the Curtiss Flying Service. *(George C. Dade Collection.)*

239. An interesting lineup of Curtiss commercial aircraft in 1929: the "Condor," "Kingbird," "Thrush," "Robin," "Carrier Pigeon II," and "Fledgling." *(Glenn H. Curtiss Museum.)*

239

CONDOR   KINGBIRD   THRUSH   ROBIN   CARRIER PIGEON II   FLEDGLING

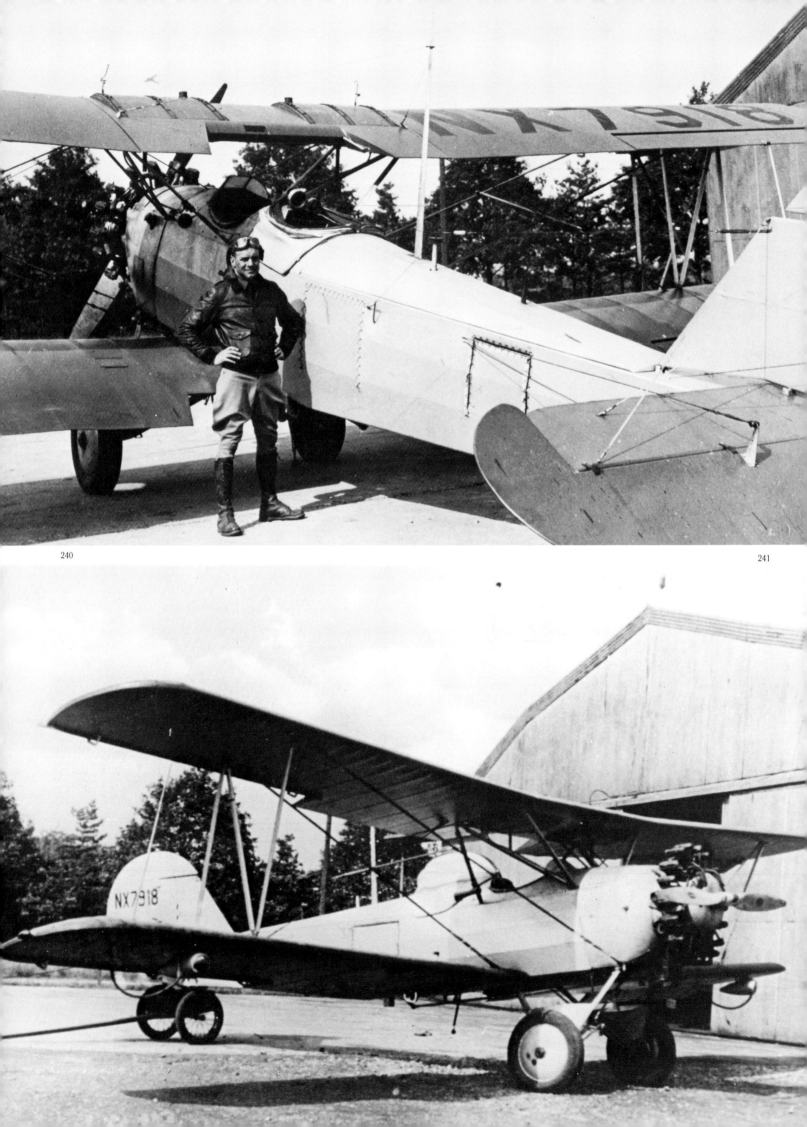

240–242. One of the last great breakthroughs in aviation technology occurred on September 24, 1929, at Mitchel Field: Lt. James H. Doolittle took off in his Consolidated NY-2 biplane, navigated a fifteen-mile course, and landed, all while flying under a hood and unable to see where he was going. This feat—the first deliberately "blind" flight— was made possible by the Sperry Gyro Horizon and Directional Gyro with which his plane was fitted. Lt. Ben Kelsey acted as check pilot. The importance of this accomplishment cannot be overrated: fog and darkness had finally been conquered for all time. *240, 241:* Doolittle and his plane at Mitchel Field at the time of the blind flight. *242:* A closeup of Lt. Doolittle (1896–   ). As Lt.-Col. Doolittle he distinguished himself in World War II, particularly when he led a surprise air attack on Tokyo in April 1942, for which he received the Congressional Medal of Honor. As of this writing (1989), Jimmy Doolittle is alive and well and living in California. *(Photo 240: National Air and Space Museum. Photo 241: Cradle of Aviation Museum. Photo 242: Nassau County Museum Reference Library.)*

243. In 1929, women aviators began to band together as a group with common interests. This photograph, taken on November 2 at Curtiss Field, Valley Stream, shows 22 of the 26 women pilots who met there to form The Ninety-Nines, an international organization of women pilots named from the number of charter members (some of whom soon responded by mail). Membership has grown by more than sixtyfold in the sixty years of the organization's existence. The five women in the front row here are (from left to right) Viola Gentry (with the flowers), "Teddy" Kenyon, Wilma L. Walsh, Frances Harrell, and Meta Rothholz. Seated in a semicircle around them are Neva Paris, Mary C. Alexander, Betty Huyler, Opal Logan Kunz (face hidden), Jean D. Hoyt, Jessie Keith-Miller, Amelia Earhart, Marjorie May Lesser, Sylvia Anthony Nelson, Dorothea Leh, Margaret O'Mara, Margery Brown, Mary Goodrich, Irene Chassey, Olivia "Keet" Mathews, E. Ruth Webb, and Fay Gillis. *(Courtesy of Ruth Dobrescu, The Ninety-Nines Inc.)*

243

244

245

246

244, 245. The Curtiss "Tanager" at the Guggenheim Safe Aircraft Competition, Mitchel Field, in the fall of 1929. Along with the interest in speed, efficiency, and commercial viability of aircraft in the 1920s, there was a growing interest in safety. This prompted financier Harry Guggenheim to offer a $100,000 prize for the safest airplane. The winner was the Curtiss "Tanager," designed by engineers T. P. Wright and Robert R. Osborn. This remarkable plane could maintain level flight as slow as 30.6 mph without stalling, take off in still air within 300 feet, and land with a run of as little as 90 feet. After clearing a 35-foot-high obstacle in the contest, the Tanager was able to land and roll to a full stop in 295 feet. Several advanced engineering devices made the plane highly maneuverable, extremely stable, and almost impossible to send into a tailspin. Top speed was 111 mph. The Tanager was an inspiration to all subsequent designers of safe aircraft. *(Both photos: Thomas Foxworth Collection.)*

246. A police air base for the New York City Police Department Air Service Division was established at North Beach Airport, Astoria, Queens (now the site of La Guardia Airport), on December 21, 1929. At the opening ceremonies (in the photograph) the police airplane "P.D. 1A," a four-place Loening amphibian biplane, was christened. *(Grumman Corporation.)*

247. This unimpressive building on Railroad Avenue (Brooklyn Avenue) in Baldwin was the first home of the Grumman Aircraft Engineering Corporation. In these modest quarters the founders, Leroy Grumman and Jake Swirbul, began in 1929 by manufacturing special floats with wheels for the conversion of Navy scouting planes into amphibians. In 1931, Grumman moved to a hangar at Curtiss Field, Valley Stream, and in 1932 to a former Fairchild plant in Farmingdale. Finally, in 1937, Grumman moved to Bethpage, where it has remained to this day (1989), the largest employer on Long Island. The Grumman Corporation distinguished itself during World War II by producing some of the most famous and effective Navy fighter planes. It has continued as one of the nation's major manufacturers of aircraft (see photos 292 and 293). (Photo taken January 1930.) *(Grumman Corporation.)*

248. Not content with his round-trip coast-to-coast flight, Capt. Frank Hawks (left) piloted a towed glider, the *Texaco Eaglet*, from San Diego, California, to Roosevelt Field, in early April 1930, taking 36 hours, 47 minutes, to make the 2,860-mile flight. The photograph was taken after landing at Roosevelt Field, April 6. Towed gliders later served an important function in World War II. *(National Air and Space Museum.)*

249. Once the use of parachutes for safety became widespread, parachute jumping turned into a sport in itself. On May 18, 1930 (not May 17, the date on the photograph), five thousand spectators watched twenty jumpers leap into the air in quick succession from a Curtiss "Condor" flying high over Roosevelt Field, establishing a world record for the number of chutists in the air at once. The event was filmed in progress by Armand Lizotte, one of the participants. Kneeling at the far right in the photograph is Henry "Buddy" Bushmeyer, the organizer of the mass jump. *(Nassau County Museum Reference Library.)*

248

249

250

251

252

250–252. The *Southern Cross* in July 1930 (location of *photo 250* unknown, probably Dayton, Ohio). This is the same plane, piloted by Sir Charles Kingsford-Smith, that made the first flight from the United States to Australia in 1928. On June 24, 1930, the *Southern Cross* left Ireland for the United States with a crew headed by Kingsford-Smith. *Photo 251* shows the Fokker trimotor monoplane after it had landed at Roosevelt Field a few days later. *Photo 252* shows it shortly after departure from Roosevelt Field on July 2, headed over Long Island for Chicago, with Oakland, California, as its final destination. *(Photo 250: National Air and Space Museum. Photo 251 courtesy of The Queens Borough Public Library. Photo 252: Frank Strnad Collection.)*

253. Stuntman Billy Bomar hangs from a strut of a New Standard D-24, with Manhattan below and Brooklyn in the background, in the summer of 1930. Such stunts are prohibited today. *(Robert Snowden Collection.)*

253

254

255

254. The *Point d'Interrogation* ("Question Mark"), the Breguet XIX biplane of Dieudonné Costes (1892–1973) and Maurice Bellonte (1896–1984), at Curtiss Field, Valley Stream, September 2, 1930. Having taken off from Le Bourget Field, Paris, 37 hours, 18 minutes earlier, these daring French aviators had just completed the first nonstop east-west, Paris-to-New York flight, paralleling in reverse Charles Lindbergh's epoch-making flight three years before. Owing to unfavorable prevailing winds, the east-west crossing actually posed a challenge greater than that faced by Lindbergh. Today, the magnitude of either accomplishment is difficult to grasp for a generation accustomed to safe, routine trans-Atlantic airline flights. Appropriately, Lindbergh was on hand to welcome the successful airmen, along with a mob that overran the airfield in a frenzy comparable only to that with which the "Lone Eagle" himself had been greeted in Paris three years earlier. *(Nassau County Museum Reference Library.)*

255, 256. As superintendent of the Texas Company's (Texaco) Aviation Division, and the oil company's chief test pilot, Capt. Frank Hawks repeatedly took advantage of the opportunity to set flying records—and then break his own and everyone else's records—in some of the most advanced planes of his day. His *Texaco No. 13* was a streamlined low-wing Travel Air "Mystery Ship" monoplane powered by an air-cooled, high-compression, supercharged 400-hp Wright "Whirlwind" J-6 engine. The radio, the gasoline-and oil-testing devices, and the full set of Pioneer instruments made the plane a virtual flying laboratory. The cockpit, cowling, and windshield were designed by Hawks himself. From August 1930 through the next few years the plane covered 125,223 miles—fueled exclusively by Texaco gasoline, naturally! *255:* Capt. Hawks over Los Angeles, August 7, 1930. On that day he flew from Curtiss Field, Valley Stream, to Glendale Airport near Los Angeles in the record time of 14 hours, 50 minutes, 43 seconds. Six days later, on August 13, he made the return trip—again in record time—taking 12 hours, 25 minutes, 3 seconds. *256:* Capt. Hawks, inspecting an oil sample, beside his *Texaco No. 13* at Floyd Bennett Field, Brooklyn, late 1930. *(Photo 255: George C. Dade Collection. Photo 256: Texaco, Inc.)*

257, 258. In May 1931, the U.S. Army Air Corps First Provisional Air Division staged air maneuvers in the Northeast. Six hundred sixty-three aircraft participated, the greatest concentration of military aircraft flying in formation as a unit anywhere in the world up to that time. Some of the planes that participated are shown at Mitchel Field *(photo 257)* and Roosevelt Field *(photo 258)*, May 22, 1931. *(Both photos: Carl "Slim" Hennicke Collection.)*

259–262. The 1930s were the era of the great flying boats—mammoth passenger-carrying seaplanes intended generally for transoceanic service. The largest flying boat of its day, the Dornier "DO-X," arrived in New York from Europe on August 5, 1931. It had begun a slow journey from Friederichshafen, Germany, in November 1930, traveling via Amsterdam, England, Lisbon, and the Canary Islands. The 169-passenger vessel had a wingspan of 157 feet and was powered by twelve engines in pairs. *259:* Flying past the Statue of Liberty.

260: Flying over lower Manhattan. *261:* In the Hudson River, off lower Manhattan. *262:* The DO-X at its final New York destination, Glenn Curtiss Airport, North Beach. (Often called North Beach Airport and the site of what is now La Guardia Airport, this field in northern Queens is not to be confused with Curtiss Field, Valley Stream, in western Nassau, or the old Curtiss Field, Garden City, which had been merged with Roosevelt Field in 1929.) *(Photos 259 and 260: Dornier Company. Photo 261 by Rudy Arnold; National Air and Space Museum. Photo 262: Carl "Slim" Hennicke Collection.)*

263. Glenn Curtiss Airport (North Beach), New York, in 1931. The enormous Dornier DO-X may be seen at the bottom, center. *(The Port Authority of New York and New Jersey.)*

264. The same site today, now La Guardia Airport, one of the New York metropolitan area's three major commercial airports. (Photo ca. 1985.) *(The Port Authority of New York and New Jersey.)*

273

275

273. Amelia Earhart standing on the wheel of her Lockheed "Vega" at Floyd Bennett Field, June 30, 1933. Some thirteen months earlier, on May 20–21, 1932, she had used another Vega to make the first solo trans-Atlantic flight by a woman, from Harbour Grace, Newfoundland, to Culmore, Ireland (flight time was 14 hours, 54 minutes). On January 15, 1935, she used the Vega shown in this photo to become the first person, man or woman, to fly alone the 2,408-mile stretch of the Pacific Ocean from Hawaii to Oakland, California (in 18 hours, 15 minutes). A little-known fact is that the same dependable Pratt & Whitney "Wasp" engine that carried Miss Earhart safely across the Atlantic in one Vega performed the same task from Hawaii to California in the other Vega. *(Photo by John F. Czajkowski and John J. Ziolkowski.)*
274. One of the 24 Savoia-Marchetti S-55 flying boats in Jamaica Bay at Floyd Bennett Field, July 19, 1933. This fleet of modern seaplanes, under the command of Italian Air Force Gen. Italo Balbo, had recently flown from Ortebello, Italy, to the "Century of Progress" exposition in

Chicago, had just completed the first leg of its return flight, and was now headed back to Italy. *(Photo by William Fleming; Frank Strnad Collection.)*
275. Wiley Post (1899–1935), famed around-the-world flier, at Floyd Bennett Field in his Lockheed "Vega" *Winnie Mae,* shortly after having landed there just before midnight, July 22, 1933. Post had just become the first to fly solo around the world, covering 15,596 miles in 7 days, 18 hours, 49½ minutes. His Vega—one of the great record-setting planes—was powered by a supercharged Pratt & Whitney "Wasp" engine. Having two years earlier circled the globe with Harold Gatty in the same plane, Post became the first person to fly around the world twice. In 1935, Post's spectacular flying career was cut short when he was killed, along with noted humorist Will Rogers, in an air crash in Alaska. The *Winnie Mae* is now on display in the National Air and Space Museum, Washington. *(Photo by John F. Czajkowski and John J. Ziolkowski.)*

276. In the 1930s, Floyd Bennett Field in Brooklyn was the starting point of many a notable trans-Atlantic flight. Here the *Joseph Le Brix*, the Hispano-powered Blériot 110 monoplane of Paul Codos and Maurice Rossi, is being readied for a flight to the vicinity of Baghdad on August 5, 1933. When Codos and Rossi landed at Rayak, Syria (now Riyaq, Lebanon), two days later, they had established a world's nonstop distance record of 5,657 miles. *(Photo by Rudy Arnold; National Air and Space Museum.)*

277. Racing pilot and aircraft designer Maj. Alexander P. de Seversky in the cockpit of his Seversky SEV-3 amphibian float plane at the National Charity Air Pageant, Roosevelt Field, October 8, 1933. Maj. de Seversky had just established a new world speed record for amphibian planes, averaging 177.79 mph. *(John Drennan Collection.)*

278. An aerial photograph taken the following year captures a full view of Seversky's SEV-3 over lower Manhattan. The advanced design features of this plane were later embodied in a number of other Seversky aircraft. Maj. de Seversky (1894–1974), a Russian-born naturalized citizen of the United States, had been the first to design an all-metal amphibious plane. *(EDO Corporation.)*

276

279

280

279. The Bellanca monoplane *Warsaw* (or *City of Warsaw*) at Floyd Bennett Field on June 28, 1934. Aviators Benjamin and Joseph Adamowicz and H. Hoiriis took off in this plane on that day and, after stopping in Newfoundland, France, and Germany, ended their trans-Atlantic flight in Thorn (Toruń), Poland. *(Photo by John F. Czajkowski and John J. Ziolkowski.)*

280. The value of aircraft for police operations was recognized very early. This Nassau County Police Department Air Division's Stinson "Reliant," photographed at Roosevelt Field, September 1, 1935, was used to fly a New York State Police trooper and his bloodhound down from the Hawthorne barracks upstate to help search for a missing person. Det. Patrick Shanley of the Missing Persons Bureau and police pilot Jack Bishop stand at the left; Det. Leroy Husser of the Warrant Squad is at the right. The Nassau police have continued to operate their Air Division to this day. *(Photo by Arthur Lembo; Nassau County Police Dept.)*

281. Like commercial planes, military aircraft continued to be improved during the 1930s. The Grumman F3F-1 "Flying Barrel," shown here at American Airport, Farmingdale, in early 1936, was assigned to the VF-5B Squadron on the aircraft carrier U.S.S. *Ranger.* The "Flying Barrel" fighters were among the most popular military aircraft of their day. The design of the fuselage eventually evolved into that of the famous F4F "Wildcat" fighter of World War II fame. *(Grumman Corporation.)*

282

283

282–284. On September 2, 1936, Henry T. "Dick" Merrill, the celebrated Eastern Airlines pilot said to have led a charmed life (but who also had more solid flying experience than any other airline pilot), and Harry Richman, the noted entertainer and an amateur pilot himself *(photo 282)*, left Floyd Bennett Field in the Vultee V-1A *Lady Peace* bound for London. Navigation problems forced them down at Llwyncelyn, Wales, 175 miles from London, but still they had crossed the Atlantic nonstop, covering the 3,300 miles in the record time of 18 hours, 38 minutes, at an average speed of 210 mph. After refueling, they flew on to London. On September 15 they commenced a return flight from Southport, England, to New York. This time problems largely stemming from Richman's lack of flying experience caused them to make a forced landing at Musgrave Harbour, Newfoundland, 1,200 miles from New York. Undaunted, they continued their flight and returned to New York. Although they had not achieved their original goal, Merrill and Richman had still made the first round-trip trans-Atlantic airplane flight (that is, without touching down on islands in the Atlantic). The photographs show Merrill and Richman at Floyd Bennett Field with the *Lady Peace* on the day of their departure for England. *(All photos by Rudy Arnold; National Air and Space Museum.)*

[156]

285. Miss Eleanor Holm (the famous swimmer and later the wife of Billy Rose) breaks a champagne bottle on the propeller of a T.W.A. Ford Tri-Motor, inaugurating Air Express service from Glenn Curtiss (North Beach) Airport, October 20, 1936. *(Photo by Rudy Arnold; National Air and Space Museum.)*

286. Al Williams with his Grumman G-22 *Gulf-hawk* at Roosevelt Field, March 14, 1937. The G-22 was a civilian version of the F3F fighter. Williams, sales manager of the Gulf Oil Company and a former Navy racing pilot (and U.S. Marine), was a familiar sight at airshows around the country with his *Gulfhawk* racing planes. *(Photo by John Drennan; George C. Dade Collection.)*

287

288

287. Imperial Airways Empire Short flying boat the *Cavalier* at Port Washington after arrival from Bermuda with 14 passengers, June 16, 1937. This marked the inauguration of regular passenger service between New York and Bermuda, operated jointly by Imperial Airways and Pan American Airways. *(Photo by John F. Czajkowski and John J. Ziolkowski.)*

288. On June 25, 1937, Richard Archbold and crew made the first nonstop transcontinental flight in a flying boat, traveling from San Diego to North Beach Airport in 17 hours, 3 minutes. Their plane, a Consolidated PBY-1 "Catalina" named *Guba,* is shown here at North Beach after landing. *(Photo by Rudy Arnold; National Air and Space Museum.)*

289. During the first week of July 1937, Pan American Airways made the first west-east survey flight across the North Atlantic with a Sikorsky S-42B "Clipper III," shown here anchored at Port Washington. This survey flight laid the groundwork for regular trans-Atlantic service to Europe in 1939. *(Photo by John Drennan; George C. Dade Collection.)*

289

290. Air commuter service is older than most people think. For years, this Grumman G21-A "Goose" shuttled wealthy business executives between Long Island and Wall Street in downtown Manhattan (where this photograph was taken on July 9, 1937). One of the most successful amphibious planes ever built, the "Goose" is still being flown commercially. *(Photo by Rudy Arnold; National Air and Space Museum.)*

291. On August 17, 1937, Lufthansa's four-engined Blohm and Voss HA 139V-1 seaplane *Nordmeer*, catapult-launched from the S.S. *Schwabenland* in the Azores, landed at Port Washington with the first seaplane-carried pay-load brought to New York. *(Photo by Rudy Arnold; National Air and Space Museum.)*

292. The airfield and factory of the Grumman Aircraft Engineering Corporation, Bethpage,

looking northwest, in 1937, just after moving to this location from Farmingdale. Residential development in this part of Nassau County was still relatively sparse. *(Grumman Corporation.)*

293. The same scene, thirty years later (1967), almost every square foot of space having been developed. Grumman continues to flourish and is now (1989) the largest employer on Long Island. *(Grumman Corporation.)*

294. Weather-forecasting technology has advanced so dramatically that it takes satellite pictures and five-day forecasts to impress us now. Fifty years ago this sight was equally impressive: the Army Air Corps' Douglas BT-2 *Weather Flight* taking off from Mitchel Field with meteorological instruments—the state of the art in weather forecasting when this photograph was taken late in 1937. The two hangars on the left, incidentally, are of the same type and on the same flight line as those which now (1989) house the Cradle of Aviation Museum. *(Photo by Rudy Arnold; National Air and Space Museum).*

295. Howard Hughes (center), William P. Lear, and Sidney Nesbitt doing some "hangar flying" at Roosevelt Field, ca. 1938. Lear was a manufacturer of aeronautical instruments and, later, of the famous Learjet. Nesbitt (in the white suit) was a pilot employed by Lear at the time. The eccentric Hughes, known at that time for his casual attire, is seen here dressed with uncharacteristic conventionality. *(Photo by John Drennan; George C. Dade Collection.)*

296. Howard Hughes (the famous aviator and multimillionaire who later became notorious for his mysterious behavior) and four-man crew with their twin-engine Lockheed 14 *New York World's Fair 1939* at Floyd Bennett Field, July 10, 1938. Three days, 19 hours, and 14 minutes after takeoff (shortly after this picture was taken), they landed in the same place, having flown a 14,672-mile course around the world via Paris, Moscow, Omsk, Yakutsk, Fairbanks, and Minneapolis. They set a speed record for the New York-to-Paris flight as well as one for circling the globe. Much of Hughes's flight had been "blind," demonstrating the efficiency of modern air-navigation instruments. (The crew included Lt. Thomas F. Thurlow, copilot and navigator; Harry F. Connor, navigator; Richard R. Stoddart, radio engineer; and Edward Lund, flight engineer.) *(Photo by Rudy Arnold; National Air and Space Museum.)*

297. This striking aerial photograph shows the extent of the crowd that welcomed Hughes and his crew on returning to Floyd Bennett Field on July 14. *(Photo by Rudy Arnold; National Air and Space Museum.)*

298

299

300

301

298. On August 13, 1938, Capt. Alfred Henke and a crew of three landed at Floyd Bennett Field in a four-engined Focke-Wulf FW-200 "Condor," completing the first successful east-west nonstop flight from Berlin to New York. Leaving on the same day, they made the return flight in record time, simultaneously completing the first Berlin-New York round trip. *(Photo by Rudy Arnold; National Air and Space Museum).*

299. On July 17, 1938, Douglas Corrigan (1907–), a pilot and mechanic who had helped build the *Spirit of St. Louis*, took off from Floyd Bennett Field in his Curtiss "Robin," headed for Los Angeles—or so he had declared. Twenty-eight hours and 13 minutes later, Corrigan landed at Baldonnel Field, Dublin, Ireland. His last-minute turnaround earned him the byname of "Wrong Way" Corrigan and led to a book and a feature motion picture. His eight-year-old Robin J-6 monoplane had been purchased for only $325. This photograph was taken at Roosevelt Field on August 14, after Corrigan's return to Long Island. Fifty years later, Corrigan, now living in California, still owns his Robin. *(Photo by John Drennan; George C. Dade Collection.)*

300, 301. Harriet Quimby, Elinor Smith, and—most famous of all— Amelia Earhart were only a few among many distinguished women fliers (often called "aviatrices"—plural of "aviatrix"—in those days). One of the most outstanding was Jacqueline Cochran. She made a late beginning, having learned to fly only in 1932, at the Roosevelt Aviation School on Long Island. Only five years later, in 1937, she won in the women's division of the Bendix Transcontinental Trophy race. In that year she also established the women's national speed record for 100 kilometers (296 mph) and the women's international speed record (293 mph), and also established a nonstop record between New York and Miami. In 1938 Miss Cochran again won in the women's division of the Bendix race, a transcontinental race between Burbank, California, and New York. *300:* Maj. Alexander P. de Seversky and the Seversky AP-7 racer he designed, flown by Jacqueline Cochran to win the 1938 Bendix Trophy (although she ended her flight at Floyd Bennett Field, this photograph was taken in Burbank, California, September 2, before she took off). *301:* Another view of Miss Cochran and her Seversky racer, number *13*, which she flew in 1938 to win the Bendix Trophy. Her flight from California to New York set a women's west-east record of 10 hours, 27 minutes, 55 seconds. *(Both photos: Republic Aviation Corporation and Frank Strnad Collection.)*

302. By the 1930s, heavier-than-air flight had developed a rich, colorful history. Over a 36-month period from 1935 through 1938, aviatrix and artist Ailine "Pat" Rhonie depicted a portion of this history in a fresco mural she painted on a 1,500-square-foot wall of Hangar "F" at Roosevelt Field. In all she portrayed 268 types of aircraft and over 500 aviators in the period 1909 through 1927. The mural was removed before Hangar "F" was torn down. Now owned by The Long Island Early Fliers Club, it is on loan to the Nassau County Cradle of Aviation Museum at Mitchel Field. *(National Air and Space Museum.)*

INDEX

*Numbers refer to **pages,** not specific captions.*